The  **NO-NONSENSE GUIDE** to

WORLD FOOD

Humanity has lost its place within the biosphere as technology seems to give us mastery over the planet. But we remain profoundly biological beings as dependent on clean air, water, soil and energy and biodiversity as any other animal for our health and well being. The challenge of our time is to re-insert ourselves back into the natural world to recognize the complete unsustainability of the modern world.

As globalization obscures locality of ecosystems and communities with brands and logos, the best way to recognize our true nature and needs is food. Every bit of our nutrition was once alive and we incorporate the fractured carcasses of plants and animals into our own bodies. What species do we consume, where, how and by whom were they reared and harvested, what was the ecological footprint of the food? Books like this get us started in our thinking and our actions.

Dr David Suzuki
Science broadcaster, host of globally-syndicated
The Nature of Things since 1979.

About the author
Wayne Roberts is a leading North American writer, activist and practitioner in community food security. Author and columnist for *NOW* Magazine, he's on the board of the Community Food Security Coalition and Food Secure Canada, and coordinates the Toronto Food Policy Council, the most respected city food group in the world.

Acknowledgements
Like a meal, a book should begin with thanks for blessings received: from mentors Herb Barbolet, George Ehring, Janice Etter, Debbie Field, Harriet Friedmann, Ellie Kirzner, Rod MacRae and Alison Blay Palmer, from Mark Winne and Pamela Roy who offered a place to hide and write in Santa Fe, my friend Michael Berger who kept me company on many research trips, ever-wise Leslie Toy who managed the shop at the food council, Adele Bonofiglio-Martins who helped with charts, dogged researcher James Kuhns, Anika, who joined me on farm holidays and kept me centered, Jaime, who helped me understand Brazil and sent great notes of support, and life partner Lori, whose presence helps me understand commitment and spirituality. I am so lucky. Thank you all.

Other titles in the series
The No-Nonsense Guide to Animal Rights
The No-Nonsense Guide to Climate Change
The No-Nonsense Guide to Conflict and Peace
The No-Nonsense Guide to Fair Trade
The No-Nonsense Guide to Globalization
The No-Nonsense Guide to Global Terrorism
The No-Nonsense Guide to Human Rights
The No-Nonsense Guide to International Development
The No-Nonsense Guide to International Migration
The No-Nonsense Guide to Islam
The No-Nonsense Guide to Science
The No-Nonsense Guide to Sexual Diversity
The No-Nonsense Guide to Tourism
The No-Nonsense Guide to the United Nations
The No-Nonsense Guide to Women's Rights
The No-Nonsense Guide to World Health
The No-Nonsense Guide to World History
The No-Nonsense Guide to World Poverty

About the New Internationalist
The **New Internationalist** is an independent not-for-profit publishing co-operative. Our mission is to report on issues of global justice. We publish informative current affairs and popular reference titles, complemented by world food, photography and gift books as well as calendars, diaries, maps and posters – all with a global justice world view.

If you like this *No-Nonsense Guide* you'll also enjoy the **New Internationalist** magazine. Each month it takes a different subject such as *Trade Justice*, *Nuclear Power* or *Iran*, exploring and explaining the issues in a concise way; the magazine is full of photos, charts and graphs as well as music, film and book reviews, country profiles, interviews and news.

To find out more about the **New Internationalist**, visit our website at
www.newint.org

The 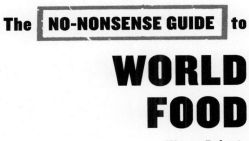 to

WORLD FOOD

Wayne Roberts

The No-Nonsense Guide to World Food
First published in the UK in 2008 by
New Internationalist™ Publications Ltd
Oxford OX4 1BW, UK
www.newint.org
New Internationalist is a registered trade mark.

Series editor: Troth Wells
Design by New Internationalist Publications Ltd.
Cover image: Market stall, Morocco. John and Lisa Merrill/Corbis.

Type by Avocet Typeset, Chilton, Aylesbury, Bucks.

Printed on recycled paper by T J Press International, Cornwall, UK who
hold environmental accreditation ISO 14001.

British Library Cataloguing-in-Publication Data.
A catalogue record for this book is available from the British Library.

Library of Congress Cataloguing-in-Publication Data.
A catalogue for this book is available from the Library of Congress.

ISBN - 978-1-904456-96-4

Foreword

A *No-Nonsense Guide to World Food* couldn't be more timely, especially given the great deal of rubbish being served to a public hungry for answers about their food. One of the common themes, which the food industry has been very keen to promote, is this: 'If we just choose the right things at the supermarket, all will be well.'

That's the kind of nonsense that this book has none of. After all, if the answer to the problem of our food is 'shopping', you've got to wonder what the question was. The surge of interest in food comes at a time when people around the world, particularly in poorer countries, are thinking about food with unprecedented sophistication, organization and creativity.

Take, for instance, the work of Via Campesina international peasant movement. It's one of the world's largest social movements with, by some estimates, up to 100 million members, in rich and poor countries, comprised of the world's poorest farmers and landless workers. They have been at the wrong end of our collapsing industrial food supply for decades, and so they know better than most what works and what doesn't. They've come up with a new vision for a worldwide future for food. It's called 'food sovereignty'.

It's a vision with some fairly clear ideas about what needs to happen so that small farmers can survive, that the environment is maintained, and that there is global justice. But food sovereignty embodies perhaps the most important lesson from years of struggle around food and agriculture: the best way to arrive at a balanced, just, and sustainable food system is to have a democratic conversation about it. The power should be in all our hands and, too often, it feels like it isn't. One thing that makes the idea of food sovereignty daunting is the fact that we've never really had a democratic conversation about food. The way our food comes to us has been shaped by corporations and governments, international institutions and oligarchs. It doesn't feel like we have much to say in the bigger debate. And the number of questions that we might begin such a conversation with are, frankly, a little overwhelming: where should I shop?, what should I eat?, what can I do to help farmers overseas?, what's a food mile and should I care about them?, can the whole world really eat organic?, what are we going to do about eating in cities?

The book in your hands not only has the answers but, better yet, the questions to ask in a further, and richer, democratic debate about our food. It's a debate that Wayne Roberts' powerful book will prime you for. The conversation and the road ahead is not easy, but it's one whose rewards could not be sweeter.
Raj Patel
Author of *Starved & Stuffed: Markets, Power and the Hidden Battle for the World Food System*

CONTENTS

Introduction

LIKE MOST THINGS in my life, I stumbled into food activism without knowing what I was getting into. I thought I was making a strictly political and technical decision. The environmental movement was stuck back in the mid-1990s, unable to get beyond criticizing governments for not doing enough, and unable to engage ordinary people in efforts to move to a positive environmental agenda. I got a feeling that food could offer a way ahead, for the simple reason that eating demands that individuals make food decisions several times a day. Transportation systems and energy systems don't do that; here, your only choice is to take or leave what's offered. So we should be able to move people along with food, I reasoned, and create some kind of movement that could demonstrate what a vibrant green movement could do.

To learn something about food, I proposed writing a book with Rod MacRae, a real food policy wonk who worked for the Toronto Food Policy Council, and my wife Lori, a senior broadcaster ready to jump ship and throw her lot in with environmental food activism. Doing that book, *Real Food for a Change*, is when I got bit by the food bug and got to really feel the issue and love everything about it. Food became great fun, and a great passion, as well as good positive political organizing. And it gave me insights into how issues connected that I'd never got from other issues I'd been active around. Among other things, it helped me feel the world as connected, and to make a commitment to do something that could contribute to confronting food problems globally.

That was 10 years ago, and nothing much has changed, except that in time I joined the Toronto Food Policy Council, and have been a professional food organizer for eight years, most of them pretty tough slogging. I was happy enough with my work, enjoyed doing a regular food column for *NOW* Magazine in Toronto, was content with my vow not to write another book, and liked being immersed in leadership posts with the Coalition for a Green Economy, Community Food Security Coalition and Food Secure Canada.

But then my wife and I went to visit a yoga school in India. While there, I got into a discussion with one of the volunteers about Islam and he told me I should read this great book – *The No-Nonsense Guide to Islam* – I could read in two hours. Two hours later, I told him I wanted to do a book in the same series because it would force me to boil down what I had learned and allow me to share it with the young people who were flooding into the food movement. So here I am: right in the thick of the action of building a local and sustainable food movement, and trying to do that with a big global picture in my head. Life is rich, and it's great to be part of a movement based on the joy of sharing abundance, which for me is what the food movement is about.

Wayne Roberts
Toronto

1 I eat, therefore I can

The problems we experience can often be linked to an invisible food system that is 'hidden in plain sight'. When we become aware of this food system, new ways of understanding food controversies and smarter ways of solving food problems start to become clear.

FOOD IS A hot topic these days for two very different reasons. One, there are so many troubling food problems to get upset about. Two, there are so many exciting food projects to get inspired by. Welcome to a discussion that affects everybody and invites everyone to make a difference.

So far, most food debates have been wired to hot buttons marked Either/Or. Choose either healthy or snack foods, good fats versus bad fats, high carb or low carb, alkaline rather than acidic diets, raw more than cooked, local not global, organic against chemical, protected as opposed to free trade, free market versus subsidized, vegan instead of carnivore, heritage seeds over genetic engineering, slow rather than fast, cooked from scratch instead of convenience packaging, fair trade rather than exploitative discounts, traditional versus modern, sustainable as opposed to unsustainable, gourmet instead of cheap, left against right. It's an impressive, if forbidding, list of possible food fights.

This book is your guide out of this door-on-your-right/door-on-your-left discourse about food choices. My training as an advocate of food policy changes is to recommend a transitional approach of continuous improvement, encouraging people to work together to start moving forward, rather than delaying by 'turning the perfect into the enemy of the good' and holding off on first moves until everything is just so.

'I'd rather work with a hundred farmers to cut their pesticide use in half than see just one farmer go totally off pesticides,' says my dyed-in-the-wool organic friend Rod MacRae, who started up the Toronto Food Policy Council before I became its co-ordinator. Creating opportunities to improve food is easier than most people think because of the possibility of bursting heroically through open doors with programs making use of both 'low-lying fruit' and 'unused capacity'. I'll discuss these two opportunity powerhouses in the final chapter, but for the time being, let's not think that meaningful food improvements are as difficult as the powers-that-be make them look.

Food systems

I am patient with continuous improvement in everyday actions because I am also guided by a global and long-term perspective toward transforming 'food systems'. The concept of food systems, central to this book, is unusual among food writers, who mostly deal with specifics such as diets, nutrition, organics, vegetarianism, and so on. I see food systems operating in much the same way as the body's circulatory system, nature's ecosystems, the educational system, the solar system, or the capitalist system, where each part is most deeply understood in relation to the whole. And so it is with most food choices, which are rarely fixed in their impact, but have a different effect depending on the system they're part of. Organic farming, for example, has a different significance in a commercial agriculture system geared to exports of specialized products than it does in a self-reliant agricultural system where diverse foods are sold to neighboring communities. Likewise, meat means different things in rocky areas where free-range livestock eat wild grasses, than it does in fertile areas where livestock have corn and soybeans brought to their barn stall.

The creative tension within this book comes from bearing two seemingly contradictory guiding principles about food in mind: on the one hand, an analysis that draws attention to all the invisible strings pulled in a food system; on the other hand, a deep belief in the power of individuals, communities and governments to introduce modest but meaningful food improvements that can inspire system changes.

A long, wide load
'To start the global task to which we are called,' says rural sociologist Jack Kloppenberg, 'we need a specific place to begin, a specific place to stand, a specific place to initiate the small, reformist changes that we can only hope may some day become radically transformative. We start with food.' Caution, the warning on the food tractor-trailer says: long, wide load.[1]

Modernist is the name I give to the food system governing today's world. Many have heard that word used to describe the engineers, architects, designers, planners, bureaucrats, business executives, conservatives, liberals, socialists, imperialists and anti-colonialists of the 1950s. They thought humans had the world by the tail, and that they could mobilize the technologies, organization and command-and-control devices to conquer obstacles to material progress in the same way they mobilized to defeat the Depression of the 1930s and Nazis of the 1940s. Agronomists, food companies, food security visionaries and many consumers during the 1950s came out of the same mold. Technological triumphalism and treatment of food as an industrial commodity drive this food system in a manner akin to the solar system's laws of gravity and laws of entropy.

'Fusion' is the name I give to an emerging world food system, which has stirred many debates and alternative visions since the 1990s. Fusion doesn't qualify for an -ist like Modernist because Fusion movements are as diverse and eclectic as fusion cuisine, featuring unlikely combinations of ingredients and styles from indigenous peoples of South America, peasants from Asia and Africa, and 'cultural creatives' (open-minded, experimental and somewhat non-conventional types of people) from North America, Oceania and Europe. The common ground for people engaged with Fusion themes and actions is treating food as a public good, valuing food as a cultural more than an agro-industrial product, and respect for food as a spiritual expression of how life is grown, recycled and connected, rather than constructed and deconstructed. Patterns akin to those that govern 'edge ecosystems', where meadow meets forest, salt water meets fresh, desert canyon meets river, underlie this system.

News agenda

This book's emphasis on conflicting food systems doesn't fit well with media reports, which usually present different news stories – about livestock diseases, childhood obesity and diabetes, rural depopulation, drastic declines of wild fish, rising prices of basic foods, deepening problems of famine and hunger, or increased pollution from food transportation and packaging, for example – as if each is its own self-enclosed story, with no systemic connection to others. Nor does this book's system focus sit well with government framing of food issues, which usually assigns food problems to government departments that have a specific duty related to agriculture or rural development or health or economic development or fisheries, as if there are no common food security or food system themes, and no possibility of resolving two related problems at once with joined-up thinking. Nor does a food system focus sit well with health and medical professionals, academics and charity leaders; their claims for funding and career advancement are based on specialized credentials and departmentalization of issues, rather than generalist skills that allow them to cross borders and partner with others to help communities address system issues.

Despite resistance to system approaches, a review of typical stories and non-stories of the last decade screams out that food is subject to system-wide problems, not just random series of unrelated mishaps. A survey of various impacts of Modernist food production methods suggests that the entire lifecycle runs against the grain of human need and harmony with Nature.

The bad news starts with Nature, what the media, government and establishment charities portray as 'the environment' – as if the environment is a world 'out there', like foreign affairs, and not indispensable human habitat, the goose that lays the golden eggs which people depend on for food. Few people learn that food production is one of the world's dirtiest industries, doing more damage to more territory than logging, mining or heavy industry. Likewise, the relationship between food and global warming – from farm fertilizer to post-dinner fart, as City University of London's Tim Lang sometimes puts it, today's gassy foods are responsible for over a third of global warming emissions – has been kept from public view and off the activist agenda until recently. The ability of farmers to harvest sunlight to grow plants, together with the ability of plants to store carbon underground in their roots, makes farming a natural-born carbon-neutral industry. Nevertheless, the belated recognition of the potential to make agriculture a leader in climate protection qualifies as one of the fossil fuel lobby's great successes in forestalling effective action against global warming.

Elsewhere on the environmental non-news beat, few if any planners have insisted on a Plan B in the event that damage to Nature's fertility – through overfishing, soil degradation, excessive irrigation, climate chaos or lack of plant and livestock genetic diversity – threatens future food productivity and security. It takes a powerful taboo against system awareness to keep such environmental stories censored and out of the public eye.[2]

Growing and eating food

Proceed from Nature to check in on the untold stories of 1.1 billion farmers, farm workers and fishers, members of the world's largest occupational groups. About 170 million food producers are child laborers, which speaks to the poverty and mistreatment subsidizing low food prices. Farming has the highest rate of bankruptcy and suicide of any occupation. Agriculture accounts for half the world's toll of workplace deaths, with 175,000 lives a year sacrificed to improper equipment management and abuse of farm chemicals. Over the last 40 years, the low incomes, irregular employment and harsh working conditions that were once the lot of rural farm laborers spread to cities, where workers who process, pack, deliver, sell, prepare or serve food are all part of most towns' biggest employment sector. A $6.4-trillion-a-year food economy that sells a necessity of life impoverishes more people than any other economic sector.[3]

I eat, therefore I can

After nature and workers, keep on trucking to eaters, the food system's clients. Though the food industry is commonly described as one where consumers are king, client service has to be ranked low when one person in six on the planet is a candidate for chronic disease as a result of excessive marketing that encourages over-eating. The global advertising budget for the food industry in 2001 was $40 billion, which is more money than the gross domestic product of 70 per cent of the world's countries. At the other end of the spectrum are under-served customers, one person in seven who suffers from severe undernourishment. Over 5,000 children die every day from diseases brought on by hunger, despite the bounty that produces ample calories for all in most countries.

Then check out governments. They spend billions every year funding self-canceling subsidies at the beginning and end of the food cycle. At the front end, governments in wealthy economies pay hefty subsidies to farmers and fishers who provide cheap food, supposedly a precondition of good health. At the back end of the food cycle, governments pick up most medical bills related to poor diets. Diet has joined tobacco and inactivity as one of the Big Three chronic killers of the age, even though diet, unlike tobacco and inactivity, has every potential to prevent diseases, including a third of all cancers.[4]

Doing the thing right

Government expenses at both the production and health end of the food cycle suggest the scope of a suppressed business story on food – astonishingly low 'allocative efficiency'. This food system ranks high in the minds of most economists, business executives and government officials for its efficiency at 'doing the right thing', producing, moving and selling lots of food. But allocative efficiency is about 'doing the thing right', getting the right goods to the right people at the right price. That job is done poorly when the potential of children is stunted by hunger, or when productive adults lose mature years to chronic diseases caused by food abuse. Governments tolerate allocative inefficiency in the food system when they support intensively managed livestock in 'factory barns', believing this to be cost-efficient and competitive. Based on his work with Veterinarians without Borders, David Waltner-Toews explains the recent emergence of 132 animal diseases with capacity to infect humans; it just happens, he says, that intense crowding of animals is ideal for handling animals at low cost, but equally ideal for the spread of infectious disease. 'Small farms have outbreaks; big farms breed epidemics; globalization of big farms creates pandemics,' Waltner-Toews writes. This is a very costly form of allocative inefficiency.[5]

When a food system performs poorly on many levels affecting many kinds of stakeholders – whether they be rich or poor, North or South, animal, vegetable or mineral – the resulting dysfunctions need to be understood in relation to one another, and not treated as if each dysfunction is isolated. The relationship identified in this book, as shall be seen, is to a complex Modernist global food system from the 1950s, which morphed into a one-dimensional 'McModernist' cheap food variation after the 1970s and a hyper-discount Wal-Modernist variation after the 1990s. At the root of this Modernist system was a set of technologies that can be described as a 'third industrial revolution' – technologies that allowed food production, processing and retailing to be fully industrialized. Industrialization created some problems flowing from the fact that food is no better suited to mechanization than are sex, love, art, education, health, religion or anything else that's close to body or soul. Problems from that bad fit have been magnified and compounded by what economists call a 'market failure', and by what political scientists call a 'governance failure'.

Many critics of the contemporary food system blame its problems on domination by one or other group of large corporations that work both ends – producers and consumers – against the middle, calling all the shots and hogging all the money. By comparison, the critique presented in this book emphasizes market failure: the inability of any leader in the food sector to develop a lens, ethic or set of public purposes (human health and environmental sustainability, for example) that can provide worthy mission statements and overall goals for all participants in the sector, as well as consistent, comprehensive and even-handed regulations and guidelines from governments. Many countries have a fisheries, agriculture, rural, health, environmental or employment policy and strategy. But if Wales and Scotland succeed in their 2008 efforts, they will be the first national governments in the world to adopt a comprehensive food policy – at this late date, over 200,000 years since humans started eating, an astonishing indication of failed governance as well as market failure. Any system with a governance failure so severe that it hasn't developed a statement of purpose will get the supersized corporations it deserves, not the human-scaled companies that people need.

Trust the complexity
Notwithstanding many 'worst of times' stories, today's food scene also has a 'best of times' excitement to it. 'Authentic' is one of the new values, to be expected in

affluent countries where availability, reliability, price and convenience are often taken for granted, and people start looking for qualities that are personally meaningful. Authentic is also valued in low-income countries, where the taste of real food is still a fresh memory cherished in the culture. Farmers' markets are part of this authentic scene. Bursting with sights, sounds, smells and chatter of real food being bought and sold by real people in real places, they offer an alternative to antiseptic and impersonal supermarkets and an opportunity to add vitality to urban streets and parks. Talk *terroir* to me, say the earthy gourmets who want to savor the climate, stewardship and culture expressed in a food's taste.

Chefs are becoming celebrities and campaigners, restoring the artisanal dignity of working with honest food and the sense of public obligation associated with the food craft. Tough customers be damned, discriminating shoppers want values as well as value for their money, creating new markets for fairly traded coffee, tea, chocolate and humanely raised livestock. 'Locavore' was new word of the year in 2007, describing customers who favor food that hasn't gone the distance. Ethical labels detail all the just, local and sustainable qualities fit to print, guiding people who practice a new form of direct economic action, the 'buycott', a deliberate favoring of one product, rather than the more negative boycott, a refusal to buy certain products. The food scene in many cities is full to busting with experiments by social entrepreneurs, co-ops, community agencies and non-governmental organizations (NGOs). Community gardens, green roofs, community kitchens, farm-to-school meal programs, Seedy Saturday heritage seed exchanges, farmers' markets, cool restaurant districts, slow food banquets, food policy councils and city food strategies are the talk of the town.

The emerging cohesive food movement is the most recent entry on the list of people power social movements since the 1790s era, which fought in turn for free speech, votes for the poor, votes for women, an end to slavery, rights to join unions and strike, national independence, social security, peace, environmental protection, women's and minority rights, and so on. Although food prices occasioned many a tumultuous protest and farmer unrest caused many a political rebellion, there was never a unified and well-rounded food movement that brought all participants to the table. Perhaps that's only happening now because successful food activism requires blurred lines that allow easy movement from personal action to informal group action to community group action to entrepreneurial and government actions – which in turn require a range of grassroots capacities that has only recently matured in global civil society. Just as the indigenous peoples of the South Pacific had scores of words for distinct forms of rain they dealt with, and the Arctic Inuit had scores of words for different kinds of snow they worked with, emerging cultures may be coming to a stage when we can develop scores of words for distinct but loose-fitting forms of collaboration that nurture, consume and honor food.

Connect the world

Connection and joined-up thinking are overarching themes which feed into a comprehensive Fusion system. 'Once upon a time everyone thought the world was flat,' said an open letter (which I helped write) signed by leaders of Toronto food organizations prior to a fall 2007 provincial election. 'Figuring out that it was round changed how we saw everything. Now the next revolution in perspective has taken hold – the world is not just round, it is connected.' The global village communicates through foodways, not just communications and computer webs, which means, the letter continues, 'this global food village must be connected by conscience and fairness – to other villages, to our environment.'

Food activists in the Global South are often leading the way, asking for solidarity, not aid or Western development models. Cubans have learned how much food can be grown in cities, and how many can be well fed without fossil fuels or pesticides. In Sri Lanka, the public health department of Colombo promotes food and herb production in shantytowns to provide income for stay-at-home mothers and support traditional plant-based medicine. Brazil and Nicaragua are pledged to achieve Zero Hunger in five years, a big step up from the UN goal of halving hunger by 2015. Farmers in Africa and Central America organize co-ops that link with Northern consumers so they can enjoy a cup of hope by capturing more of the value of quality coffee, tea and chocolate.

At a parallel conference to the World Food Summit in Rome in 2002, the global peasant organization Via Campesina encouraged food security organizations from the Global North (including befuddled people like me, attending my first international meeting) to adopt the demand for 'food sovereignty', in opposition to World Trade Organization-style free trade, thereby putting local and community control of food systems on the global policy agenda. At the same conference, agro-ecology – a made-in-the-South strategy for linking the growing of food, medicine, fuel and fiber for self-reliant and environmentally friendly communities

I eat, therefore I can

– emerged as a distinctive method for reconfiguring agriculture. Just one year later, major governments from the Global South confronted Northern governments at a World Trade Organization meeting in Cancún, Mexico, and refused to accept token reforms to a trade system that forced governments of the South to be open to subsidized Northern exports, while governments of the North continued to block entry to Southern imports. As of early 2008, the WTO has not figured a way out of the North-South stalemate.

The Force is with Fusion

In short, there's a whole lot of shaking, norming, storming, informing and re-forming going on. Although the Fusion alternative is qualitatively smaller than the Modernist system, the Force is with Fusion. This is where the youth, energy and initiatives are. Modernists are on the defensive, lacking both big ideas and small, rousing little enthusiasm – check the lackluster and questionable results from Bill Gates throwing his billions at 1950s-style Modernist schemes – attracting few new adherents, facing resistance and setbacks on every front. Even Wal-Mart, the icon for Discounted Modernism, is taking organics into the mainstream and refusing to carry genetically engineered milk. Fusion is the system to watch.

Does Fusion have the right stuff to grow into the future and nourish the world with good food? Speaking about his best-selling 2008 manifesto on food, US author Michael Pollan admitted to a Toronto banquet crowd that his book's mantra – 'eat food, not too much, mostly plants' – lacks the battle cry of earlier manifestos. 'It's not exactly Workers of the World, Unite,' he said, but if people change their eating habits, 'much of the world will change, and not just in the food sector.' He encouraged people to 'vote with your fork' because 'food is one of those areas where the personal is political', and simple acts such as cooking fresh produce from a local store can 'help reclaim control of the food system' from global multinationals. This is a case when doing the right thing is easy, Pollan argued. 'There aren't many places in the world where the right thing to do is the most delightful thing,' he said.

There are several powerful messages in Pollan's remarks. First, he argues that alternatives to the status quo exist, and work well, especially to improve health – a value that allows him to speak to mainstream Americans, he believes. Second, Pollan states that the alternatives are within reach of most people, and require only simple actions, such as buying and cooking whole foods.

'The alternatives are there for the taking,' is how Raj Patel describes the same idea. Author of another looming bestseller, *Stuffed and Starved: Markets, Power and the Hidden Battle for the World's Food System*, Patel is referring to the fact that food doesn't need the complex and expensive infrastructure which products such as steel or cars require. Food transactions can be quite simple and direct – farmers bring their goods into town and townspeople buy the goods at a market, for example – until owners of infrastructure such as supermarkets make relationships complicated by having farmers produce specific ingredients and consumers buy meals prepared from combinations of ingredients. As soon as consumers free themselves from their self-inflicted servitude to established shopping and cooking formats, the power to cut supermarkets down to size will be in their own hands.

Third, Pollan emphasizes what I call The Power of One, the mainspring of energy among many young food activists, a far cry from earlier generations of radicals who envisioned individuals acquiring importance only as part of huge collectivities such as the proletariat or the state. Fourth, Pollan exudes positive energy. Although he doesn't hesitate to criticize delinquent corporations and government agencies, he wants people to join in demonstration projects, not just demonstration protests. Joy, not hairshirts or self-righteousness, is the prescribed additive of his food revolution.

The gaping hole in Pollan's do-it-yourself projections, quite typical of Americans of all political stripes – they come from a country, after all, where the only progressive identification to check off on Facebook is 'Very Liberal' – comes from an inability to imagine government playing any positive role to protect or enhance the public interest. His advice to vote with a fork mixes metaphors terribly, because voting is what people do as citizens participating with others in a collective act of self-government. In a democracy, people don't vote with their dollars or forks, but as persons with rights and duties.

Government role

Jeanette Longfield, co-ordinator of the British food coalition Sustain, is more attentive to the crucial role of expansive government food policies, thanks to her organization's experience animating citizen input into London's food strategy, a 10-year plan with an $8 million budget adopted in 2006 to increase the amount of healthy, safe, sustainable and universally accessible food coming to London from the surrounding countryside. She's flexible about where people should start the public policy process.

'Getting it going, moving networks into action, is more important than getting it right,' she stressed during a 2007 trip to update people from Toronto on her London campaign. Adapting a Toronto foundation report on food organizing, Longfield identifies four sets of actions as essential to public policy reform. First is to 'change the conversation'. More often than not, changing the conversation means learning the language of the groups that need to become involved; mayors, for example, probably relate more to food issues that address tourist attractions, jobs for at-risk youth, revitalized streets and pollution reduction – big issues that big-city mayors are often held to account on – than to nutrition. Longfield tries to open the conversation by calling food a 'latchkey issue', which unlocks a multi-purpose strategy to boost local employment, raise the stature of local restaurants, reduce pollution from long-distance transit, protect nearby farmers and farmland, and improve food access for people on low incomes – the latter being a fave of London's first mayor, 'Red Ken' Livingstone.[6]

Authors of the Food and Agriculture Organization's annual report for 2005 adopted a similar approach to conversation-changing when they talked up anti-hunger investments as the key to successes with United Nations Millennium Development Goals (MDGs). Moving on hunger advances the agenda on all eight campaign goals – eradicate extreme poverty, promote universal primary education, empower women, reduce child mortality, improve maternal health, combat infectious disease, ensure environmental sustainability, and encourage global development partnerships. That says a mouthful about the need for conversations that raise the profile, priority and utility of food issues.[7]

To translate the latchkey concept into economics lingo, food is an 'intermediate good', which, like electricity, creates indispensable value by what it energizes and facilitates. Most intermediate goods – money, roads and postal delivery are other examples – are considered so essential to social well-being and national security that governments support and regulate them more than they do mere commodities. The way food has been traditionally regulated bespeaks the fact that governments have put it in the wrong column of economic activity. When London adopts a food strategy, it helps change the global food conversation by

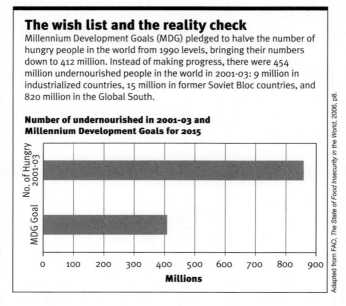

The wish list and the reality check

Millennium Development Goals (MDG) pledged to halve the number of hungry people in the world from 1990 levels, bringing their numbers down to 412 million. Instead of making progress, there were 454 million undernourished people in the world in 2001-03: 9 million in industrialized countries, 15 million in former Soviet Bloc countries, and 820 million in the Global South.

Number of undernourished in 2001-03 and Millennium Development Goals for 2015

Adapted from FAO, *The State of Food Insecurity in the World*, 2006, p8.

identifying food as an intermediate good that has strategic significance for word-class cities.

Sharing the aims

Having broken the ice by changing the conversation, Longfield proceeds to stage two: 'bridge the divides.' That's a tall order in the food sector, which has a more than reasonable share of territorial feuds, jurisdictional moats, occupational snobbery, academic infighting, interest group silos and policy-wonk tunnel vision. There's a legacy of farmers feeling insulted by environmentalist remarks, and a tradition of people on low incomes resenting 'yuppie foodies', to name only two sets of bad feelings to overcome. But if grassroots and membership organizations don't get their act together on their own, they will be divided and conquered, and no-one with innovative or far-reaching food policy plans will get anywhere. Slow Food has made a valuable contribution in this regard by redefining eaters as 'co-producers', whose constructive feedback to producers is a crucial part of the creative food process. As a result of bringing disparate groups together, Sustain's website sports the names of some 100 unlikely partners and strange bedfellows who sponsored its national campaigns to improve school meals and limit junk food marketing to kids. The proof is in the pudding that divides can be bridged with proper care and handling.

Conversation is flowing, divides are being bridged, at which point Longfield gets down to business with stage three: 'rebuilding the middle'. The Modernist food system, especially its cheap food version, followed a scorched earth policy toward traditional infrastructure built in the days of local food provisioning. Supersized supermarkets built their own supply chains, and saw no need for local or public warehouses and processors that also served their competitors, mom and pop groceries. Nor did national supermarkets or processors like local farmers' markets that operated on public space. These interests made their money as 'middlemen', turning farm products into consumer purchases, and saw no value to bringing people at both ends together.

Rebuilding the middle requires both hard and soft infrastructure. Hard infrastructure includes local warehouses, canners, freezers, brewers and slaughterhouses, as well as revived main streets anchored by full-service independent grocers. Soft infrastructure includes listservs/mailing lists, food e-Bays, food policy councils that link farmers, customers and well-wishers. Skill-building, career planning and on-the-job training will be the order of the day, as farmers learn about relationship marketing and new revenue streams – such as school fundraisers that feature local delicacies; farm-to-school meal programs; school-to-farm tours, or sales to community kitchens that provide street vendors with fresh and local snacks (one of the purposes of Brazil's early community kitchens).

From table to farm

As much as anything, soft infrastructure includes measures to humanize relations between farmers and consumers, and overcome the corrosion of a common humanity from the habit of seeing ourselves strictly as producers or buyers of commodities. I often meet farmers who talk about nearby cities as their 'market'. We're not your market, I try to explain; we're new immigrants from Pakistan, we're single moms, we're seniors at risk for heart disease, we're university students living on our own; if you think of us as an impersonal market, we'll do the same to you and buy our food from somewhere cheaper; so let's use food as a chance to get to know and appreciate one another as people before we do business.

In short, rebuilding the middle requires food producers and consumers to think beyond the linear logistics of 'from farm to table' and meet in a new two-way middle where 'from table to farm' is equally important. Soft infrastructure also bleeds into policy reform, the next phase, because specific food safety standards need to be defined for the small scale of local and fresh goods.

Conversation, bridging and middling under way, the foundations for Longfield's stage four, policy reform, are in place. It's remarkable how down-to-earth food policy reform needs to be. Chefs and farmers' markets give local food glitter. Government purchasing gives it heft, creating demand that allows alternative producers to scale up. It could easily take farmers five years to catch up with orders that come in once government purchasing becomes the norm. It's about a steady diet of continuous improvement, with constant egging by media, advisors, staff and citizen groups.

To me, the London effort feels a lot like Toronto's Food and Hunger Action Committee, set up to celebrate the New Millennium and Toronto's new status as an amalgamated metropolis. I helped co-ordinate the Committee, which had politicians, civil servants and community leaders as equal members. Four action routes were agreed on unanimously in a 2001 report. *Facilitate*, as in provide free meeting rooms, space for farmers' markets, grants to start up neighborhood-scale projects. *Advocate*, as in adopt a charter of food rights to educate citizens and pressure other levels of government. *Organize*, as in help seniors and children to handle food gardening. *Innovate*, as in provide incentives for green roofs and encourage local food purchases that sustain a local, distinctive and secure food economy. Later, those of us who continued on the project added *Animate*, as in fund organizers who can go into highly stressed areas and use food activities – such as community gardens, community kitchens and farmers' markets – to breathe life, pride and community spirit into new neighborhoods.

Not much of a master plan coming from either Toronto or London, and accomplishments are humble compared to what's been done in Belo Horizonte, Brazil, or Havana, Cuba, both to be presented in coming chapters. Around the world, people are starting to work on solutions, grappling with the problems and challenges. If London, Toronto, Belo Horizonte and Havana are typical, the people working on such projects will learn to be positive and open about the process of creating opportunities for solutions at all levels. They will agree with Jeanette Longfield when she says: 'you have to trust the complexity'.

1 J Kloppenberg et al, 'Coming into the Foodshed,' in *Agriculture and Human Values*, 13, 3, 1996. **2** T Lang and E Millstone, eds, *The Atlas of Food* (Earthscan 2003). **3** T Lang, 'The Death of Food as We Know It,' *The Ecologist*, March, 2008; www.planetretail.net **4** R Horton, 'Cancer: Malignant Maneuvers, in *New York Review of Books*, 6 March 2008. **5** D Waltner-Toews, *The Chickens Fight Back: Pandemic Panics and Deadly*

I eat, therefore I can

Diseases that Jump from Animals to Humans (Greystone Books, 2007), p 104. **6** Longfield spoke to four of six orientations to policy reform identified in P Campsie, *Food Connects Us All: Sustainable Local Food in Southern Ontario* (Metcalf Foundation, 2008). **7** FAO, *The State of Food Insecurity in the World, 2005: Eradicating World Hunger – key to achieving the Millennium Development Goals* (FAO, 2005) pp 2-5.

2 Brave new food

An industrial food system helped win World War One and was a major victor of World War Two. When we understand this military-agricultural complex, we understand the idealism behind food security and the war against want, but also the tragic flaws of 1950s' Modernist thinking.

THE ROAD TO junk food, rural poverty and agricultural pollution was paved with good intentions. Often criticized as greedy and vulgar, today's global food system was created in the last months of World War Two as part of an ennobling vision to create a new world of abundance and peace. The Washington monument to US President Franklin Roosevelt features many of his later wartime statements, when he was preparing for peace. We want 'more than an end to war, we want an end to the beginnings of war', he said – the deep conviction behind the formation of the Food and Agriculture Organization in 1944, while the War was still being fought.

The belief was that rivalries leading to war came from insecurity and want, so dealing with the world's need for food was a form of waging peace. In the same time period, Roosevelt declared freedom of speech and worship, freedom from want and fear, to be formal war goals, revealing a thought pattern that wove personal, social and economic freedom into one security blanket. That's just what the United Nations Universal Declaration of Human Rights did in 1948, when it insisted its package of individual and social rights was indivisible. These lofty concepts are still invoked in the names, if not the content, of US food aid programs, such as Food for Peace. It is also carried on in the title of organizations devoted to 'food security', a phrase that comes from this era – when social security, job security, union security and old age security expressed an ethic of overcoming anxiety and scarcity by sharing life's risks and good fortune.

Food was central to this ethic, wrought while people embroiled in war were dreaming about peace. Few thought about food, war, peace, plenty and power as much as Claude Wickard, a hog farmer from Indiana who served as Roosevelt's Secretary of Agriculture from 1940 to 1945. In 1941, he already understood that 'food will win the war and write the peace'. To keep civilian morale high and soldiers fighting fit, 'the world needs vitamins and fats,' he said. He directed farmers to switch from corn, tobacco, rice, cotton and wheat, and start producing milk, cheese, eggs, pork, lard, beef, fruits and vegetables. As he witnessed government agents and farmers marshaling energy to produce what was needed, he felt 'boundless with the promise of a better world,' and dreamed of 'enough food for the whole world.' Wickard said, 'The goal is more production, more consumption, a higher national – and eventually international' standard of living. His assistant, Milo Perkins, celebrated these first farmers in world history to grow enough food for all, and believed the days when people fought over who gets what were a thing of the past. 'That's the most important material thing that's happened to the human race since the discovery of fire and the invention of the wheel,' Perkins said.[1]

Frontline food

This vision of the future was composed of: one part American Manifest Destiny; one part wartime adrenalin; one part penance for the folly of war; one part awe at the commitment, solidarity and purposefulness evoked by war; one part commitment to build a world fit for returning heroes; and one part worship of Science, which did as much as food to win the war and could do as much to win the peace. There is no denying the continuing, albeit sub-conscious, military heritage linking science, fighting, victory over enemies and food. 'Recommended Daily Allowances' and 'fortified foods', standard on food packages to this day, came early during the war, part of an effort to keep people 'strong and healthy' so they could stay 'strong and free' by adding chemical nutrients to foods that lacked sufficient punch on their own. Likewise, food guides leaned heavily on animal fats – two of the four food groups – girding muscular bloodlust with protein, calcium and iron.

Habits of speech that marshal support for the war on cancer, the battle against poverty, the fight against obesity, aggressive treatment of infections, invasive surgery to destroy disease, all bespeak the same conquering, bloody-minded and wrongheaded way of thinking about bodies, illnesses, weeds and insects. Pesticides and herbicides, rooted in the same -cide as in genocide and homicide, come from the same root misunderstanding of the link between food production and war. Some of the worst chemicals, such as the infamous DDT, 2,4-D, parathion and malathion, were developed as nerve gases or to protect troops from malaria. Peacetime purposes were found for this weapons arsenal in agriculture, with names such as Ambush, Force, Warrior, Battalion, Arsenal, Stalker, Boundary, Captain Ammo and Machete, not to mention Converge, which 'kills weeds – then comes back to get their friends', it was claimed.

'World War Two did not so much end,' writes Ron Kroese, 'as turn its guns and bombs on the land.' Often the militarist appeal had a progressive twist, as when national school meal programs were motivated in 1946 because they ensured the health and preparedness of future soldiers. Although the phrase 'military-industrial complex' is commonplace, thanks to the farewell address of President Dwight Eisenhower, himself a former top soldier, 'agro-military complex' does more to explain the cultural recesses beneath modern farming and food policy.[2]

Conflict of interest

It's also likely that the standard government assignment of food to departments of agriculture rather than of health or community development had its origin in military logistics. Assigning farming to a department of agriculture is a slamdunk, just like assigning factories to a department of industry. But assigning food and agriculture and rural affairs to a department of agriculture, as became standard, is no more natural than putting labor, consumer protection and new business development in a department of industry. The grouping of food, agriculture and rural development is flawed in logic and governance. There's a conflict of interest when one department is expected to champion and protect both farmers who sell and consumers who buy the same product, just as there's a conflict between promoting mechanization of agriculture and maintaining the size and stability of rural communities.

Logic models that checked up on assumptions of planners were developed during the 1970s, partially in response to Modernist habits of 'throwing money at problems'. Putting agriculture departments in charge of food is like throwing food at a problem which properly starts with a diagnosis of health needs, not farming possibilities or needs. The broad empire of agriculture departments only makes sense in wartime, when food is being mobilized to address the needs of armed forces – because, as Napoleon was one of the first commanders to notice, an army marches on its stomach – and to protect civilians from being starved by enemy blockades. Other than in wartime, folding food, agriculture and rural development in one department is a mechanism that ensures signals will get perpetually crossed, and that no legitimate interest gets its proper desserts.

During the 1950s, many wartime enthusiasms ripened into universal Modernism, the most hegemonic ideology of the 20th century. The belief that science and technology could liberate humans – free them from the past and its limits of ignorance, discipline of scarcity, pettiness of labor, burdens of scarcity – stirred hopes that a new generation could go where none had gone before. Modernism unified both Left and Right in both the imperial and colonial worlds. Only a minority resisted government funding that took roads, harbors, seaways and energy to areas where food and industrial production could leap forward. Few pined for the days of backward peasants and smallholder farmers. More proletarians in steel mills and car plants provided life's new essentials, while more tractors, pesticides and irrigation ensured more of the old ones.

Western Europe's rapid reconstruction after the War gave an object lesson that Big Money and Big Projects could work secular miracles. In what was christened the 'developing world', Development and Modernism were synonymous. In Egypt under Nasser and perhaps India under Nehru, the quintessential Modernist construction project – a mega dam that dominated and domesticated a once-sacred river to create electricity and irrigation for export agriculture – was blessed as a monument to modern civilization. Likewise, there was a consensus about a 'mixed economy,' in which governments played a leading role as motivators, planners, regulators, supporters and actual roll-up-the-sleeves doers. Other than for a few beatniks and disciples of Gandhi, Modernism was a future that brooked and required no debate.

Industrial farming
Modernism introduced fundamental change at eight levels of the food system, each having global significance. First, there was a revolution in how food was produced (produced being the operative word). Tractors and combines, capital-intensive equipment worthy of a heavy industry factory, became the norm in industrialized countries. Science- and engineering-intensive inputs – such as irrigation, chemical fertilizers,

Brave new world

petrochemical pesticides, specialized livestock breeding and patented hybrid or engineered seeds – became the norm in export-oriented agriculture, while industrial feedstocks such as soy and maize became central to intensive management of livestock.

Second, there was a revolution in who produced food – not the farmer down the lane or the spouse out in the backyard, but an unknown member of the global labor market.

Third, there was a revolution in where food was produced. Once containers, superhighways and seaways drastically cut the costs of transportation, the standard rule on ratio of bulk to value was overturned. It used to be thought that small and costly products were the only ones that could bear the cost of long-haul transportation; bulky and low-value products (cheap lettuce, which is over 80 per cent water, for example) suddenly qualified for long-haul transit at a minuscule addition in cost per unit.

Fourth, there was a revolution in how the food was processed before being sold: no longer in bulk bags of flour and potatoes, but in cans and boxes, usually with multiple ingredients (including preservatives), and often, as with the TV dinners and baking mixes of the 1950s, ready to heat and eat.

Fifth, there was a big change in where consumers bought food, from the farmers' market or local store to the supermarket, more recently, at the gas station, discount box store or drugstore.

Sixth came the revolution in how food was home-cooked, or rather, prepared. Household skill levels for baking from scratch or cutting a roast went down, while use of smart equipment, such as microwaves, slowcookers, breadmakers, and coffeemakers – half of them doubling as clocks and alarms – went up.

Seventh was the revolution in where food was eaten, moving from the kitchen to the TV room and, later, from the home to the restaurant.

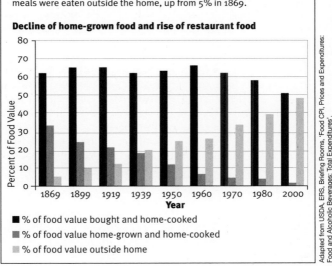

Home sweet take-out

The rise of the modern food system changed where food was grown, how meals were prepared and where they were eaten. A third of US food was home-grown in 1869, down to 1% by 2000. Almost half of meals were eaten outside the home, up from 5% in 1869.

Decline of home-grown food and rise of restaurant food

Y-axis: Percent of Food Value (0 to 80)
X-axis: Year (1869, 1899, 1919, 1939, 1950, 1960, 1970, 1980, 2000)

- ■ % of food value bought and home-cooked
- ■ % of food value home-grown and home-cooked
- ■ % of food value outside home

Adapted from USDA, ERS, Briefing Rooms, 'Food CPI, Prices and Expenditures: Food and Alcoholic Beverages: Total Expenditures'.

Eighth was the revolution in how food is eaten, or rather hoovered, scarfed or gulped. Food was once quintessentially social; breaking bread, companionship (which comes from the Latin for 'with' and 'bread'), family meals and celebratory banquets were the norm, as were rituals of thanks and grace. The Modern way, cut off from nature, tradition and intimate connections, is to eat in the car while talking on a Blackberry. All eight of these transformations got under way during the 1950s and 1960s, and each expresses at least one cardinal value of Modernism.[3]

Post-war dreams

I had a hard time figuring out what went wrong with

the Modernist dreamlist because of my fond memories
of growing up with this post-war generation. All the
moms and dads on my street had gone through tough
times during the 1930s' Depression and World War
Two, and finally got the chance to have the home,
family and neighbors of their dreams: to own a car,
take a modest summer holiday, give their kids chances
they never had, and never worry about having food on
the table. My mom and dad loved to share the good
fortune of a comfortable working-class life by working to spare children from hunger and war. After my
mom died, a peace group, the Voice of Women, held a
memorial meeting in 2007 for her and other leaders.

The meeting was hosted by Canada's wisest woman
elder, Ursula Franklin, a distinguished metallurgist
who wrote the classic critique of Modernism, *The
Real World of Technology*. Speaking without notes,
the 86-year-old Franklin described peace as 'more than
the absence of war, but the presence of justice.' I went
up to ask her for some help. If peace is more than the
absence of war, then abundance must be more than the
absence of hunger, I said. What is it? In a split second,
she said 'Balance: abundance is the presence of balance.' In a word, that's it. Modernists didn't balance
quantity with quality, strength with health, mechanization with handiwork, comfort with challenge,
consumption with engagement, mastery with humility,
abundance with sustainability. Lack of balance and
resilience explains why it couldn't accommodate the
challenges of the 1970s and why it started to come
undone after the 1990s.

Modernism of the 1950s and 1960s, it must be said,
delivered the goods in Europe and North America,
especially with food. It was plentiful, affordable,
and came in convenient and liberating ways that
previous technological shakeups didn't get around
to. Mid-century Modernism coincided with a third
industrial revolution that married science and business

to transform the way food, household and consumer goods were produced. More precisely, new technologies transformed food by producing and processing it. This technological makeover set the foundations for most food trends of the last 50 years. Ironically, this third revolution lacks the public recognition of its two predecessors, probably because it provoked so little resistance. To grasp its unique qualities, hunker down for a brief comparison with its two technological ancestors.

Revolutions, past and present
The first, best-known, and still-capitalized Industrial Revolution swept through much of Europe during the 1700s. The Industrial Revolution revolutionized food, but didn't industrialize it. The food news at that time was cheap colonial imports of sugar, tea and coffee, and shifting mealtime habits linked to urban squalor and factory hours. The first Industrial Revolution featured factory production of rough-fitting shoes and textiles, but machine tools were too imprecise to shape metals, and too clumsy to deal with the tricky maneuvers required in agriculture or the ticklish texture of most foods other than cookies.

The second industrial revolution, associated with electrification, flourished from the 1890s to the 1930s. Mass production principles were extended to disassembly lines in slaughterhouses and assembly lines for cars. But with the exception of pasteurization, trans fats, white bread and canned goods, most agricultural and food preparation tasks were too delicate and situation-specific to be mechanized. When something is described as 'the best thing since sliced bread', it is not being compared to anything that happened long ago. Pre-sliced characterless bread came on the scene in the late 1920s, a reminder that wholesale industrialization of food inputs and processing awaited technological changes almost as recent and revolutionary as the computers that have industrialized data inputs and processing.

The third industrial revolution, from the 1940s through to the 1970s, finally caught up with food. New technologies and processes cracked the codes that had kept food production from being mechanized. Electricity was taken to rural areas of the industrialized world, allowing for all manner of practical changes – think refrigeration for milk or lighting and heating of barns – that let one farmer manage more animals and crops. Weeds and pests didn't know what hit them when they were sprayed with the new generation of petrochemical pesticides. DDT, the best-known, took the bullet for the pesticide industry following the storm of environmental protest aroused by scientist and ecologist Rachel Carson's *Silent Spring* during the early 1960s. But powerful pesticides were essential to farmers who produced more food on more hectares with less labor, so substitute sprays were brought on, featuring toxins that didn't exist in nature, and which Nature couldn't break down. Automated process technologies, pioneered in the oil and plastics industries, were applied to food processing – a phrase that escaped the scorn of more contested mutual contradictions, such as military intelligence, media ethics, or Microsoft Works.

On top of better living through chemistry and electricity came new forms of business organization. The term 'agribusiness' was coined in the mid-1950s by US President Eisenhower's former Assistant Agriculture Secretary, John H Davis, and Ray Goldberg of the Harvard Business School. Until then, there were no courses that envisioned one integrated food industry from farm to table, an industrial chain in which farm products became 'inputs'. The first Harvard seminar for business executives was in 1956, and Goldberg takes pride that every US Department of Agriculture (USDA) secretary since has taken part. To keep up with bulk orders from centralized agribusinesses, Agriculture Secretary Ezra Taft Benson told farmers they had no choice but to use economies of scale to spread the costs of expensive inputs over more output. So, 'get big or get out', he told farmers. Corporate, industrialized and scientific food production became synonymous.[4]

Food system without a cause

There is no guru of Modernist Food akin to innovator Bucky (Buckminster) Fuller, who believed food production and home-building had to become as industrialized, efficient and streamlined as auto assembly, or architect Le Corbusier, who described homes as machines to live in. Small mercies. Nevertheless, several food projects provide snapshots of the Modernist sensibility toward food.

Space travel during the 1960s epitomized Modernist ambitions to break the chains that bound humans to Earth. The food provided to American space cadets was a small processed meal for man, a giant processed meal for all mankind. Russian astronauts were treated to fine cuisine that allowed them to take Russian culture into space, but the US astronauts' need for food was treated as an 'inconvenient necessity' deserving of space program inventions such as Tang, rehydrated mashed potatoes, and – a snack that has not yet been commercialized – cookies that converted urine into protein. One astronaut reported that if he added water to dehydrated peas, beans and asparagus before heating them, 'I still didn't like them, but they were a lot easier to choke down than when I added the hot water, shook up the bag and then tried to get them down.' Developed with almost unlimited budgets, this menu may explain why Modernism added little to the world's cuisine, however much it contributed to innovative food-like ingredients and substitutes.[5]

Brave new world

Supermarket surge

The supermarket burst on the food scene with typical over-the-top Modernist hype – skyscrapers, super-highways and supersonic bombs are other Modernist vanities – and typical Modernist building techniques: lots of glass, chrome, high-powered lights, straight rows. Profligate energy waste is common to Modernist designs, expressed in huge open freezers at the store matched by substantial fridges to store the purchases at home before tossing excess in the garbage. Standard supermarket props can literally be checked off any Modernist design listing: bright packages, perfect-looking produce, no odor of actual food or sign of feathers, blood or rot that might suggest the food's origin, no yelling, hawking, bantering or greetings, no haggling over price, no buskers or street people, no public property not totally controlled by the owner, and minimal artistry, enchantment or decoration, unless Muzak qualifies as music.

Abundance is the first message of the supermarket, which is why more staff are employed keeping all shelves full than looking after customers. Consumer choice is the second message. Convenience is the third, which is why supermarkets are usually attached to parking lots, and why supermarkets destroy main streets with their efforts to promote one-stop shopping. Affordability was the fourth, but has probably moved up to first or second under the pressure of discounters since the 1990s. In the UK, supermarkets almost doubled their share of the market during the 1960s, taking most sales from independents; they did not take from co-ops until the 1990s. In the US, supermarket share of food sales soared from 14.9 per cent in 1948 to 55 per cent in 1972, growth that mainly took from mom and pop groceries, specialty stores and home delivery services. By the 1970s, supermarkets were pivotal players in the food industry. They used their control over access to customers to control the entire food chain through the power of aggregate or bulk buying. They imposed their price points on processors, who imposed their price points on farmers, who did what had to be done. This was a true retail revolution, as Tony Winson, one of the first authors to identify this trend, has noted.[6]

Full-on, abundance-spreading Modernism flourished during the 1950s and 1960s. That's when global politics were defined by two factors: the Cold War between the USSR and the US, which pressured both to do nice things to vie for support from other countries; and the end of old-fashioned European colonialism, which opened possibilities for former Asian, African and South American countries to participate in 'development'. There were 'three worlds of development' – the American and European First World, the Soviet Second World, and the increasingly restive Non-Aligned Movement which came to be known as the Third World. Strategists for both US and Soviet Modernist food systems tried to jockey for political and economic advantage in this arena.

Green revolutionizing

The US had several reasons to support increases to the farm productivity of Third World, now often called 'Majority World' or 'Global South' countries. First, it thought this was the way to solve hunger problems that caused mass unrest: by 'growing the pie' so there was more for everyone, rather than fighting over slices of a smaller pie. Second, it hoped to document the superiority of US production methods over Soviet ones. Third, it hoped to capitalize on sales of industrial farm inputs (tractors, fertilizers, and so on) used by 'high input, high yield' Third World farmers.

High input, high yield agriculture came across as dull as dishwater as a campaign slogan. Then a US Government publicity flak came up with the name 'Green Revolution', who hoped this spin on high-yield farming contrasted nicely to Red (Communist) Revolution.

The Johnny Appleseed of the Modernist field of dreams is Norman Borlaug, who has received the Nobel Prize and scores of other top honors for his contributions to peace and development through high yield-farming. As a youth during the 1930s Depression who worked on public works projects for the unemployed, he took up agricultural research when he saw the connection between hunger and war. 'You can't build a peaceful world on empty stomachs and human misery,' he explained. Websites dedicated to Borlaug's reputation commonly claim that he has saved the lives of one billion people who would have starved to death without his growing techniques. Borlaug's first big project was sponsored by the Rockefeller Foundation in Mexico during the 1940s. His most famous work was in India during the 1950s and 1960s. His current work is with the Gates and Rockefeller foundations in Africa. Some see significance in the long-standing connection to Rockefeller (Standard Oil/ESSO), given the high fossil-fuel needs fostered by Modernist high-input agriculture strategies.

Modernists were famous for saying that 'form follows function'. They despised wasting energy and expense on frills that didn't add to a building's purpose. Borlaug felt the same way about plants. Their job was to increase yield for humans, the only species that apparently counted in this input-output analysis. He believed that many grain plants wasted too much energy on tall stems with no function other than to stand tall. In Mexico, he selected wheat plants with dwarf stems, which boosted grain output. In India, he worked on rice that matured quickly, producing an extra crop on the same space each year.

Yields skyrocketed under Borlaug's shock and awe demonstration of what US-sponsored science could accomplish by overcoming the old ways. Rice output doubled almost overnight. By 2001, India grew 70 million tons of Green Revolution wheat, enough to feed everyone in India 2,800 calories a day. Instead of going to the one Indian in five who is chronically hungry, the surplus grain went to a 60-million-ton stockpile, some destined for export. More than food production increases were needed to end hunger, especially in 2001, when no Soviet-sponsored Cold War competition existed.

Payback time

Since 2000, the Green Revolution piper has had to be paid. Short-sighted promotion of short-stemmed plants left less fodder for livestock, and less straw for composting manure fertilizer, depleting the land of complex micronutrients. Some fields were degraded from salt deposits in irrigation water, which is hard, unlike soft rainwater that might have been more ingeniously designed than Modernists ever gave Nature credit for.

Community relations in many areas have deteriorated as a result of infighting over access to scarce inputs, such as well water. Suicide rates for the Punjab's many indebted farmers are nightmarishly high; the Green Revolution, argues Devinder Sharma, one of India's leading agriculture critics, 'has not only turned sour, it has now turned red' with blood. *The Economist*, usually a fan of scientific bells and whistles, pronounced the Green Revolution in the Punjab, India's breadbasket, 'in retreat' and a 'catastrophe'. Two reports from the state government of the Punjab – formerly the poster child of the Green Revolution – have recommended a return to pre-Green Revolution farming methods.[7]

'Feed the world'

Food aid was another insignia of the Modernist approach to food. Following World War Two, the US played on a world stage, confronting its Cold War enemies and assisting its Cold War allies. About $13 billion in aid through the Marshall Plan helped Europe recover from the devastation of war between 1947 and 1952. On the heels of this success, the US donated billions in food aid to governments it deemed in need of assistance, almost always non-Communist ones or ones in international hotspots.

Food aid was the showpiece of US generosity but, like most charitable programs before and since, had more than its share of patronizing errors. The US felt it was called to 'feed the world', a bad metaphor in two respects. First, cattle are fed, babies are fed, human adults eat.

Second, people generally seem to have a deep preference to be proud and self-reliant when it comes to food; they may not mind someone else paying more taxes to educate their children or cover their unemployment insurance, but it cuts to the quick to depend on charity for food. Dependence is especially resented if there's suspicion that the food donor expects something in return; then there's a feeling that one country is taking advantage of another's hard times to extract something they wouldn't otherwise give. There's not much doubt that some US key players behind food aid had some deal in mind, either 'future considerations' in later purchases, or actual shifts in local diets to accommodate US exports.

Many analysts believe that food aid played the role of the Trojan Horse in Greek mythology, encouraging countries to let down their guard until it was too late; then, their own farmers were bankrupted by competition with under-priced US imports and had left their farms to find work in the city, and their own consumers had become used to the Western grain-based diet. Once a society depended on imports, it was on the commercial treadmill. US aid, says leading analyst Harriet Friedmann, disrupted subsistence economies by 'widening and deepening of capitalist relations within the world economy, by shifting vastly more of the world's population away from direct access to food and incorporating it instead into food markets.' Turning food into a traded commodity, she says, was 'a crucial aspect of proletarianization' of formerly subsistence economies turned into workshops of cheap manufactured goods for export.

Trading with aid

Until food aid was developed, most North American grains were sold into Europe. Countries in Asia, Africa and South America remained self-sufficient in grains before World War Two. After the war, the US Government worked with its grain farmers to export as much surplus as possible. In 1950, for example, over 60 per cent of US exports were financed as aid. By 1956, US aid accounted for a third of the world wheat trade, much of it directed to countries encouraging people to leave their farms and work in factories. By 1968, poor countries of the world took 78 per cent of US exports. Wheat and similar grains had become the export products of industrialized countries of the Global North, and two standard routes to modernization of former colonies – through export agriculture, or import substitution – were closed. The ongoing legacy of US food aid, Friedmann argues, is colonial dependence on high-priced grain imports, painfully truer in 2008 than when she published her study in 1982.[8]

Speeches trumpeting high-yield agriculture are still the comfort food of choice at food industry get-togethers. In Chicago, which is known as the buckle of the Midwestern corn and soy belt, a blogsite sponsored by the Federal Reserve Bank of Chicago reports on a 2007 conference on production agriculture. Featured speakers explained how research was central to the US ability to feed the world. A major presentation by economist David Oppedahl reviewed the signposts of progress: farm output has more than doubled since

Brave new world

1948, despite huge reductions in cropland, farm workers and farmers; soy and corn output has doubled since 1964; each farmer increased hourly output 12-fold between 1950 and 2000; food prices since 1948 rose at less than half the rate of general prices; the farmer's share of the food dollar in 1997 was 21 cents.

Many defenders of pesticides or genetically engineered seeds dress their cause with rhetoric from post-World War Two Modernism. Militant defenders of the faith include Dennis Avery, the Hudson Institute author of – I'm not making this up – *Saving the Planet with Pesticides and Plastic: the Environmental Triumph of High Yield Farming*. Other good old boys wax eloquent about Genetic Engineering (GE) as the savior of poor farmers and consumers despite widespread evidence to the contrary. There is evidence, for example, that yields are better with organic, that the low-input costs and demands of traditional seeds are more helpful to low-resource farmers, and that actually-existing GE is in fact limited to products that yield little health benefit.[9]

McModernism

But the spell of post-war Modernism was broken during the 1970s. In 1971, a hallmark strategic assessment of the economy led President Richard Nixon to promote 'green power' as part of the US bid to become 'breadbasket of the world'. This was premised on the US becoming worldbeaters in the arena of cheap agriculture, turning over the Modernist applecart with its now-obsolete idea that all nations could become partners in sharing abundance. The subsequent drive to boost subsidized exports of US grains, as development sociologist Philip McMichael has documented, both grew out of and destabilized global Modernist-inspired food and development projects. It was no longer about sharing abundance and helping others to develop; it used poor countries as a dumping ground for grain surplus and source of cheap imported manufactures – a new phase of Food Modernism I call McModern.[10]

Other cracks in the Modernist consensus were revealed in 1974, during the high-profile US-sponsored international conference on famine, hunger and runaway food prices. Classics of the global food movement were written in response to the hoopla of that event. Susan George's *How the Other Half Dies* and Frances Moore Lappé's *Food First: Beyond the Myth of Scarcity* were precocious in their time and still read well today, setting out key elements of the global agenda for a different kind of food system. During the 1970s, Modernism lost its hegemonic groove and became controversial. Other food strategies seemed possible.

The bloom came off the idealistic rose in 1976, when the US opposed a UN-sponsored International Covenant on Economic, Social and Cultural Rights, which reaffirmed 'the fundamental right of everyone to be free from hunger'. In contrast to the 1940s, when personal, social, cultural and economic rights were treated as indivisible, food became, in US eyes, an economic, social and cultural right, not a human right. The US-sponsored International Covenant on Civil and Political Rights of the same year makes a vague reference to everyone having 'the inherent right to life,' without a mention of food or other bodily essentials. Preparing for the 1998 celebration of the Universal Declaration of Human Rights' 50th anniversary, Louise Arbour, UN High Commissioner for Human Rights, complains that the assumption that prosperity will look after the poor 'is a misguided view of what human rights are about.' She says: 'there's no reason to assume that prosperity will transform itself naturally into any form of social justice.'[11]

Fast forward to 2008: with over $50 billion a year stated for crop subsidies, the US farm bill influences the fundamentals of world agriculture and food practices.

The direct crop payments, in order of money received, go like this: corn, wheat, cotton, soybeans, rice, sorghum, barley, peanuts. Several things stand out in this list. All are export crops, and almost all give the US global price leadership, determining what unsubsidized smallholder farmers will be able to charge in their own countries. All crops can be produced with high levels of mechanization, reducing the disadvantage that the US might face in competition with low-wage economies, but also reducing the US jobs created by US public expenditures.

These subsidies actually encourage hollowing out of the countryside, in the US and elsewhere, by artificially encouraging large mechanized farm operations. All the crops deplete water and soil nutrients; subsidizing them violates a basic principle of resource conservation. Many, especially corn and cotton, require high levels of powerful pesticides, thereby subsidizing the poisoning of water tables. At least four – corn, soy, barley and wheat – are mainly intended for livestock and production of low-cost meat. Subsidizing these grains is a way of laundering government money to products and companies that few people would think worthy of subsidies: beer from barley, pop from corn syrup, ethanol fuel from corn or wheat, meat from raising livestock on corn and soy instead of grass and hay. By subsidizing these crops, the US Government lowers the cost of indulging in practices that are harmful to health and the environment – the opposite of sound economic planning. No fruit and vegetables, no alternative crops, and no crops grown for local markets are on this list. I call this phase of Food Modernism 'Wal-Modernism'.[12]

The original Modernist vision of the 1940s has been stripped of almost all but the language and dreamscape of US influence over global thinking and practice around food issues. The notions and institutions of combining science, planning, government commitment, public co-operation and wide-ranging human rights were discredited and dismantled during the 1990s, with the formation of the World Trade Organization, Modernism's veritable counter-revolution – Wal-Modernism. All that remains of the original commitment is high production agriculture. A system which hoped to provide bread for all settled for living on bread alone.

1 'Hunger: Cover Story,' *Time*, 21 July 1941. **2** See, for example, A Blay-Palmer, *Food Fears: From Industrial to Sustainable Food Systems* (in press, 2008); S Dean, 'Children of the Corn Syrup,' in *Believer*, October, 2003; Ron Kroese, 'How Did We Get Here: The Culture of Agribusiness,' in *Conscious Choice*, May 1999. **3** Thanks to Tim Lang, who first developed a similar list. **4** 'The Evolution of Agribusiness,' in HBS@Work Faculty Interview; www.exed.hbs.edu/assets/faculty/rgoldberg.html **5** J Levi, 'the rise of the gastronaut,' in J Knechtel, ed., *Food* (MIT Press, 2007). **6** T Lang and M Heasman, *Food Wars: The Global Battle for Mouths, Minds and Markets* (Earthscan, 2004), p 166; 'Food CPI, Prices and Expenditures: Sales of Food at Home by Type of Outlet,' in USDA/ERS *Briefing Room*, 2 July 2007; T Winson, *The Intimate Commodity: Food and the Development of the Agro-Industrial Complex in Canada* (Garamond Press, 1992). **7** V Smil, *Feeding the World: A Challenge to the Twenty-First Century* (MIT Press, 2001); R Thurow and J Solomon, 'An Indian Paradox: bumper harvests and rising hunger,' *Wall Street Journal*, 25 June 2004; www.earth-policy.org/Updates/2005/Update45_data.htm; V Shiva, *The Violence of the Green Revolution: Third World Agriculture, Ecology and Politics*, (Zed, 1991); D Sharma, 'The Collapse of Green Revolution,' at www.stwr.net/content/view/116/37/; 'Chemical generation,' at *Economist.com* 24 September 2007; 'Need to stop disastrous cropping pattern: Report,' at www.punjabenvironment.com 27 August 2007. **8** H Friedmann, 'The Political Economy of Food: The Rise and Fall of the Postwar International Food Order,' in *American Journal of Sociology*, 88, 1982. **9** http:// midwest.chicagofedblogs.org-/archives/200710/ **10** P McMichael, *Development and Social Change: A Global Perspective* (Pine Forge Press, 2000) p 64. **11** G Kent, 'Food is a Human Right,' foodnews 22 June 2004 archived at www.foodforethought.net/ ; F Williams, 'UN drive for economic and social rights,' *Financial Times* 8 January 2008. **12** L Etter and G Hitt, 'Farm Lobby Beats Back Assault on Subsidies,' *Wall Street Journal*, 27 March 2008, pp 1,12.

3 Putting food sovereignty in its place

When food is of, by and for the people, then food security lies in food sovereignty. When we understand the food traditions of indigenous peoples and peasants in the Global South, the ethic of community-based food systems and food sovereignty starts to become clear.

INTERPRETATIONS OF FOOD security are in the eye of the Northern beholder. Some understand it through the looking glass of war-related national security concerns that European, Soviet and North American countries faced during World War Two. Some liken it to income security programs that many governments introduced after that war. Some, especially in the United Nations, see secure access to adequate food at all times as recognition of human rights. Informal polling of people I know tells me that most people hear security alarms when they hear 'security', and think food security is about protecting the food supply from contamination by bio-terrorists or avian flu. I always get waved on with a smile and godspeed through airport security and US customs as soon as I say I work in public health, and am going to the US for an executive board meeting of the Community Food Security Coalition.

Ironically, the US-based Community Food Security Coalition took its name in response to concerns that many North American food activists had about possible misinterpretations of food security. During the 1990s, the term was associated with charity and foodbank donations to the poor and hungry. The term 'household food insecurity' was used by some government staff and nutritionists to distinguish the kind of hunger suffered in the industrialized world – missing several meals a month, and eating low-quality meals the rest of the time – from the life-threatening hunger suffered elsewhere. This approach was disliked because it separated rather than unified all people with food access problems, and described hunger as a household rather than a community or government problem and responsibility. So when a small band of food activists met in 1994 to form a North American coalition, Mark Winne from the Hartford Food System in Connecticut suggested they pick a name to distinguish themselves from the Government. He proposed Community Food Security Coalition. 'I put the ram in the ramadamadingdong,' he says.

Fusion-style food activists in many places across the Global North picked up that term. They like highlighting community-based programs, such as community gardens, community kitchens and farmers' markets. And they like including food issues in community planning – in government purchasing of local foods, business zoning to make quality food stores available to all, and food projects as part of school curriculum, for example.

Change of name

Then came a similar but feistier change of name from a very different place. The subject of this chapter, the name change to 'food sovereignty,' follows a long, sad story. In 1995, the World Trade Organization (WTO) came into effect with new kinds of rules on food, fishing, farming and related issues. Through most of the Global North, the WTO is synonymous with free trade, usually of cheap imports that put Northern workers out of a job. Through most of the Global

Food sovereignty

South, the WTO means a package of 'neoliberal' changes that threaten core cultural values, as well as survival and economic needs.

The full WTO package includes three changes for the worse: deregulation (an end to government laws that favor local companies or restrict competition, for example); privatization (sell-off of public lands, buying up patents of regional seeds, closing government warehouses that help small farmers, for example); and a distorted form of free trade (exports from government-subsidized farmers in Europe or North America to the Global South are allowed, but many unsubsidized Southern foods are banned in Europe or America for safety reasons). Until the formation of the WTO, no international trade body intervened so extensively in the food and agriculture policies of any country, because food was considered a public security matter that all governments needed to plan for, and because food was so central to the income levels and food access of a huge majority of the world's population.

Given that the WTO is unelected and meets largely in secrecy, this is quite an invasion of the traditional sovereignty of all countries. But in the mind of WTO negotiators, food is a commodity, and should be treated like any other commodity. No governments have any automatic right to protect their producers or consumers from brutal offshore competition, private ownership of patents, or foreign control of community resources.

The imposition of a wide range of WTO rules on global food practices is arguably the most traumatic non-military expression of the 'new world order' ushered in after the collapse of the Soviet Union and fall of the Berlin Wall in 1989. No longer able to jockey for the best trade offer made by two competing

No reason for hunger

If all citizens have the optimum amount of food for a healthy and active life, there are enough calories for everyone, even in most of the poorest countries. Hunger is, therefore, a policy problem, not a fate that people are condemned to suffer.

Selected countries where over one in five are undernourished

Country	Millions of Undernourished 2001-03	% of Population Undernourished	Available Calories Per Person
Armenia	0.9	29	2260
Bolivia	2.0	23	2220
Ethiopia	31.5	46	1860
India	212.0	20	2440
Senegal	2.2	23	2310
Thailand	13.4	21	2410
Yemen	7.1	37	2020

Adapted from FAO, *The State of Food Insecurity in the World*, 2006, pp.33-6.

superpowers, the peoples of Asia, Africa, and South America now faced one supreme überpower, the US, which had an extra free hand to reorder North-South issues. The US, on its own or through the World Bank and World Trade Organization, became much more demanding in trade and other negotiations, and much less tolerant of ideological deviations from its brand of ('do as I say, not as I do') free market economics. Many achievements won during the broadly progressive Modernist consensus after World War Two – UN support for social and economic rights, national government actions to boost food availability and access, public regulation or ownership ('command and control') of key economic levers ('commanding heights') in most national economies, Keynesian-style government spending to boost purchasing power of people on low incomes, and so on – were phased out in one country after another. It is hard to underestimate the impact on 'customer service' to the world's poor countries of having global competition replaced by global monopoly. This change in the balance of world forces led to further degeneration of the global food system – from Modernist during the 1950s to McModernist during the 1970s, to Wal-Modernist since the 1990s.

WTO rules

When WTO rules went into effect, farmers and peasants in the Global South were shell-shocked by the collapse of prices in their home markets, as they were forced to compete against heavily subsidized exports from Europe and the US. Through organizations such as Via Campesina (loosely translated, the Peasants' or Countrypeoples' Way), they demanded 'Take Agriculture out of the WTO' as a way to restore some of the protection farmers, farm workers and peasants enjoyed before 1995, in days when food was still exempted from global trade rules.

The food needs of people had to come first, the WTO critics argued: before politics, ideology or markets. Arguing that the right to decide on food production and distribution matters was a basic right of independent countries, many food activists in the Global South called their goal 'food sovereignty', two words that had rarely run into each other before. Food sovereignty campaigns, it was hoped, might block the North American- and European-controlled World Trade Organization from usurping food independence, or, equally important, might pressure national governments to stop using the WTO as an all-purpose excuse for doing nothing to improve food security – a rarely examined effect that the WTO cultivates among lackadaisical governments around the world, which journalist Linda McQuaig has brilliantly dubbed 'The Cult of Impotence'.[1]

In 2002, the global peasant organization Via Campesina took the food sovereignty term to a Rome international citizens' gathering paralleling the World Food Summit. During several days of militant public marches and conference displays of peasant outrage against Northern governments, the only interruptions happened during key moments of soccer games, when the meeting hall was briefly evacuated to watch the action. The new term, expressing the new power and dynamism of the Global South in the international food movement, was adopted as the international position of progressive food organizations. For a brief time after, I represented North America on the steering committee of that emerging organization. Fellow activists introduced me to the profound differences in the ecology, crops, food production methods and people's history of countries in the Global South and North, differences that give richer meaning to food sovereignty than the words themselves express to most people, and which this chapter will try to convey. In a field that's short of big bang ideas, food sovereignty is a big bang idea, so I'd like you to know it from the inside out.

One way to interrogate food sovereignty is to look at the Why, Where, What and How of food production in the Global South, and to ask how it intersects with the developing Fusion style in the Global North. Although this leaves out the excruciating details of Who is sticking it to farmers and eaters around the world (to be discussed later), it reveals the cultural, historical, spiritual and ecological depths that food sovereignty comes from, not just the harsh realities it responds to.

Food sovereignty

Hopefully, this Why, Where, What and How organizing device reveals four powerful trends behind food sovereignty: the inherent Global North bias behind the way ostensibly global organizations deal with food and agriculture; the inherent conflict of interest bedeviling international food-related organizations, such as the World Bank and Food and Agriculture Organization, when they deal with the Global South; the geographically and socially determined need for unique food regimes in the Global South; the powerful cultural, ethical and spiritual inspiration behind food sovereignty thinking.

QUESTION 1: WHY GROW FOOD?

The differences that cause a global conflict over food come up as soon as someone asks: why would anyone (in their right mind) grow, gather, hunt or make food? A simple question, but in the 1990s it took professional training to come up with the answer acceptable to established authorities: to sell it, preferably into export markets. That wasn't a common view before. People worked the land, it was thought by most, because it gave food for them to eat; it was a good place to raise a family, and offered good honest work fulfilling a crucial public need. Farming was primarily a way of life that connected with great forces in the universe, not simply a way of making a living. This belief added ethical vehemence and cultural vitality to the way Southern peasants responded to their economic suffering during the 1990s. This foundation beneath Global South protest converged with more eclectic expressions of similar values throughout the Global North, as Fusion-style food thinking took hold. Both Northern and Southern food activists agreed enough on the Why and Why Not of agriculture to share a common starting-point of food sovereignty – the specialness of food and food production.

After the 1990s, people who thought about food and farming from an economic perspective made no bones about boosting food sales. 'The key policy challenge,' the World Bank's report for 2008, *Agriculture for Development*, says, 'is to help agriculture play its role as an engine of growth and poverty reduction.' Profitable exports can bring in foreign cash to pay farmers and lift them out of poverty, the Bank argues. This presumption that rapid economic growth is the only goal for agriculture and the best way to end hunger riles Vandana Shiva, one of India's best-known critics of globalization, who calls it one of the leading 'myths' that keep people poor. 'People are perceived as "poor" if they eat food they have grown, rather than commercially distributed junk foods sold by global agribusiness,' she writes.[2]

Banking on loans

It's possible that authors of World Bank reports have not received the memo on export fetishism stating that stores are not the only places in the world to find food. More likely, authors of World Bank reports are caught in a conflict of interest that prevents them from seeing the obvious. The World Bank is in the business of loaning money to projects that can pay off a World Bank loan, plus interest to cover the salary of the World Bank author. Growing food in a subsistence economy may solve a local hunger problem, but it does not solve the World Bank's problem of finding good debt risks. The Bank, which calls itself an anti-poverty organization, never comes clean that it is in the money-lending business, and offers advice to match. That's a dicey governance problem. It highlights the need for people in low-income countries to assert their food sovereignty so they can make their own decision on the merits of the case to focus on cash crops for export or food crops for their own population.

The UN's Food and Agriculture Organization is saddled with a similar conflict in mandate to the World Bank's. It is supposed to represent food sellers as well as the needs of the hungry poor, who mostly earn less than two dollars a day and lack the means to be good customers. Wearing its fishmonger's hat, the FAO's 2002 report, *The State of Food and Agriculture*, cheers the good news of growing demand for 'fish products'. Sales of Southern fish to Northern markets 'reveal the potential of these products for revenue generation,' the FAO notes. But the FAO overlooks how exports to affluent countries inflate fish prices in local markets. George Kent, an expert in human rights and the fishery, worries that sales into the global market subvert, rather than enable, poor people's right to access fish, which used to be 'the poor person's protein'. From a Southern perspective, export markets do not provide food, but take it away, by privileging Northern money over local need for a local resource.[3]

Food for eating

What if someone says the reason to grow food is to eat it, especially in rural areas where most extreme poverty and hunger is concentrated? The government of Malawi, a small landlocked country in Africa, did just that. It had to defy pressure from the World Bank as well as European and US aid agencies, which favored concentrating on exports, but the Malawi Government decided to try to leverage modest government funds to help people grow their own food.

Five million of Malawi's 13 million people relied on

international emergency food aid following the failure of their 2005 corn crop.

Newly elected President Bingu wa Mutharika resolved not to go begging for food again, and started plans for food self-reliance. He knew that soil infertility was the immediate cause of the 2005 crop failure. He knew that farmers lacked money to buy fertilizer. He knew it would cost the Government $58 million less to buy fertilizer for farmers than to pay $120 million for emergency food aid, as it did in 2005. So, he provided discount coupons for fertilizer. People in each village decided who would get the coupons, generally giving first priority to those most in need. Good weather and fertilizer combined to double the harvest in 2006. By 2007, output tripled, and there was enough surplus to export $120 million worth of corn. 'This is the best agrarian program in years,' says Richard Petautchere of the Malawi Economic Justice Network. 'We have the land, we have the water, we have everything but that doesn't matter if you just can't buy seeds or fertilizer,' he adds. The success of the Malawi project confirms the need to recognize a principle of food sovereignty – local self-reliance and self-rule in food matters – rather than placing authority in institutions and markets far from the scene.[4]

From the standpoint of human health, the best case for policy that focuses on promotion of local consumption of a commercial-free local resource is breastfeeding. Breastmilk is the richest and safest, but most overlooked, food resource for addressing the needs of the world's highly vulnerable eaters, infants and toddlers. It also provides an economics case study that can be learned at a mother's knee about physical, mental and emotional nourishment coming from human relationships, not commercial ones. Regrettably, few consumers of breastmilk are paying customers. As a consequence, breastmilk does not qualify as a food product or commodity, and has no impact on the GNP, the only indicator of economic well-being some economic agencies will take to the bank. Few economic development agencies include it in their evaluations of best economic practices in the food sector.[5]

Soil connections

In many cultures, especially before 1995, there was a clear understanding that there was more to food production than meets the mouth or the pocketbook. To forget how to dig the earth and tend the soil is to forget ourselves, Gandhi used to say. Most religions and spiritualities value that connection over shopping. Adam is the ancient Hebrew name for soil, while human and humus both descend from a common root in the early Indo-European language. That connection to the soil through food production can have public health, as well as personally spiritual, impacts.

Good karma in sound bodies comes from social support, personal self-esteem, competency, belonging, engagement, according to a major statement of the global public health movement, the 1988 Ottawa Charter on Health Promotion. These qualities can all be engaged in food production and preparation, and could be considered as sound reasons to encourage more people to grow food for health reasons. Understanding the human need to have a hand in making, not just consuming things, famous futurists Marshall McLuhan and Alvin Toffler forecast during the 1970s a new social type who is already a fixture of the Fusion food scene in the Global North – the 'prosumer', the producer-consumer hybrid typified by practitioners of one of the world's fastest-growing hobbies, gardening. Just because it's recreational (as in re-creation) doesn't mean the activity doesn't create food.

I experience the non-commercial Why to food production first-hand every summer, when my wife and younger daughter join me as unpaid volunteers on a working farm holiday. I watched my 12-year-old Anika jump out of her skin on our first day at Stowel Lake Farm at Salt Spring Island on Canada's west coast. The owners asked her to pick through a dug-up potato field with her bare hands to find any potatoes left behind. Can adults be asking me to play in the dirt, her eyes laughed in disbelief. On our last day, she beamed again when she was invited to help milk two Jersey cows, with a walking style that came right out of the ancient nursery rhyme about 'the cow that jumped over the moon'. One of our co-workers, typical of many young people doing short volunteer stints on farms to see if they really like farming, classified herself and friends as 'more likely inspired by Noam Chomsky than the *Whole Earth Catalogue*'. Like me, they seemed to relate to farmwork as a labor of love, what *Small is Beautiful* author EF Schumacher called 'good work'. Working on a farm with others passes Schumacher's three tests for good work with flying colors. It produces necessary goods and services, so no-one has to ask 'what's the use?'. It nourishes pride of accomplishment and empowerment. And it offers opportunities for a burst of team-spirit high, like when our crew 'blitzed' a field full of what we called Tyrannosaurus Rex weeds so the strawberries could have a fighting chance.

Natural high

Part of this joy may come from a farm variation of what psychologists call the 'biophilia thesis' – the healing and restfulness that many get from connecting with growing and tending food. The Swedes and Danes know how to work with this to increase access to nature, natural exercise and fresh food. When we visited my father-in-law's family neighborhood in Angelhome, Sweden, we took the bus to the last stop on the edge of town, walked a short while and found a 'Koloni'. At the entrance, there were showers, laundry, toilets and similar services that require electricity and plumbing. The rest of the grounds, accessible only by footpaths, divided into lots of 300 square meters, each with a cabin just big enough to store a few things and relax inside if it rained. The lot is leased for a modest yearly fee of about $100. The cabin is extra, usually purchased from the previous renter.

Food access during a time of hardship was the original purpose of the 'Koloniträdgårdar' during World War Two, but now people outdo themselves growing flowers, fruit trees, vines and vegetables as they choose; the issue is access to nature, and food is the icing on the cake. This garden campground is a monument to the ancient Nordic commitment to 'everyone's right' to access Nature. The major users of the service were people on modest incomes who couldn't afford a private cottage getaway, or who didn't have space for their own garden in the city. Provision of such Koloni is a simple, smart and cost-effective way for a public service to address both human needs to connect with the land and needs for food, an ideal near-urban service to parallel what many governments already provide for summer campers in more rural surroundings. For governments that like to talk about giving the poor 'a hand up rather than a hand-out', as well as those who believe in the value of nature appreciation accessible to families and children, this is a nice starter project. The 'hand-up' concept is a sound one, but usually requires that governments use their access to capital or assets (such as land) to make them available to people, who can use the main resource they have lots of: labor time and willingness to work if given an opportunity.[6]

French farming

Appreciation of the human need for contact with the soil comes from a famous French politician who might be considered the last person ever to question a purely economic model of farming. Edgard Pisani was the cabinet minister responsible for modernizing French agriculture and industrializing European farming during the 1960s, transforming a region with food deficits into the world's second biggest food exporter. Much later in life, he considered that he had 'badly evaluated the consequences' of the farm efficiency revolution he engineered. I met him when he was 86, still a dashing figure with his bold style and tall frame, touring North America to encourage debate on his two latest books: *A Personal View of the World* and *An Old Man and the Land*. Both books created a sensation in France because of his opposition to subsidies for farm exports, his support for environmental payments to farmers, and his plea to the world's farmers to focus on their home markets.

When Pisani was prefect of two agricultural areas during the 1940s, most farmers lived in homes with dirt floors and no electricity, phones, running water or motorized equipment. Farmers were a third of the population, and an average farmer fed 2.5 people. When Pisani resigned after 20 years of subsidizing mechanization, a typical farmer fed 15 people, and he wanted to call a stop at that. But the juggernaut couldn't stop. Today's French farmers each feed 70 people, but still rely on subsidies that boost production. Subsidies and production 'prosper together', he writes, and 80 per cent of the government money goes to 20 per cent of the highest-producing farms.

Pisani credits his change of heart to helicopter rides he took over the countryside as lead negotiator for the European Economic Community's agriculture program, which gave him an overview of the destruction of the natural and social landscape. Farmers shouldn't be subsidized to produce more food, he concluded, but to 'carry out tasks for the common good that affect the natural environment'. Because protection of humus makes agriculture a 'quasi-public service', it should be paid for, he argued. Three faces of agriculture – food production, environmental protection and support of rural society – require an end to free trade of agricultural goods in globalized markets, he says, so farmers can recover lifestyles based on 'humus and humility'. He points a long, bony finger at his favorite passage in the book, which comes from French author Antoine de Saint Exupéry: 'The Land teaches us more than all books: because it resists us.'

Such thinking as to the Why of food production provides the cornerstone of food sovereignty thinking, and informs the easy consensus that allows both Northern and Southern food activists to embrace food sovereignty as a goal and framework of global food policy.

QUESTION 2:
WHERE DOES FOOD COME FROM?
Farmers work their fields. Peasants work the land. There's a world of difference. Agriculture comes from the Latin *ager*, which means field. Romans branded bread as the staff of life and stuff of civilization itself, partly because wheat was a domesticated field crop.

When Europeans colonized much of the world after 1500, they spread a Roman-inspired agriculture based on wheat and fields. That's why Europeans had to 'conquer the wilderness', as well as the 'savages' and 'primitives' who lived in the wilderness, as soon as they began settling and ruling an area. For people immersed in Roman-based European culture, forests have to be cut and wilderness has to be conquered if civilizing food is to be had. Once food production is done on controlled fields, it's a relatively small step to make one field the property of one person who can invest in it, and to shunt common or communal property to the sidelines.

By contrast, food producers elsewhere in the world were not out standing in their fields. Many were in boats or on the beach, seeking fish and seagreens (seaweeds) in open-source, commonly managed water-ways. Many others were in commonly managed wild meadows or forests seeking food, fuel, fiber for clothes and buildings and feed for livestock. Instead of grain-based field crops, some grew root crops, well-adapted to multi-use forests. That's what happened in Brazil, home of cassava/manioc, or terraced mountainsides in Peru, home of the potato. Other societies had tree crops, source of the spices that captivated Europeans, or of fruit, nuts and beans.

When Europeans, and later Americans, imposed plantation or field agriculture on colonies, they imposed an alien form of field-based food production that did not co-evolve as a partnership connecting people, culture and land. Few have examined exactly how wrenching and brutal that change in food production methods was. Forest-based cultures and religions are different from dryland ones, for example. Community relations are different when resources are

Food sovereignty

managed communally (more common outside Europe) or privately. Environmental impacts are qualitatively different. When pioneer farmers cut down forests and plough up land, they uproot and release carbon previously stored by trees; about a third of increased global warming emissions over the past 150 years come from this one aspect of agriculture, according to the UN Environment Program report for 2007. Not least, dietary variety is profoundly influenced, with field-based economies more likely to focus on a few intensively managed crops, while non-field economies are more likely to graze and nibble on hundreds of foods and medicines.[7]

Away from the fields
With food, as with real estate, it's a matter of location, location and location. Food sovereignty comes from a place, first and most forcefully from a place in the Global South, where non-field food production has taken on the name 'agro-ecology'. The Where of food production is as important as the Why to understanding food sovereignty and where it comes from. Understanding this Southern thinking also helps anticipate trends that will resonate with agro-ecology in the North, as people find the 'wherewithal' to think about alternatives to fields, such as agro-forestry or permaculture.

About 1.6 billion people depend on forest livelihoods, according to the FAO's forestry department. Forests are equal opportunity workplaces. They don't discriminate on the basis of color, religion or formal education. They have no rules against women who bring their children to play beside them while they work, which may explain why women in India risked their lives to protect their life-preserving forest economy from loggers by 'tree-hugging'. The multiple products available from forests in different seasons make them a haven for people to fall back on whenever times are tough. Likewise, forest work has modest start-up costs – a basket to pick leaves and berries, a drill to tap sap, a knife to cut saplings are typical, nothing expensive requiring access to credit. A multiple-use forest, managed as a grocery, pharmacy, hardware and clothing store without walls, provides security for the very people likely to face hunger. Food, fiber for clothes, fiber for building, materials for crafts, fuel, medicine, fodder for livestock: it's one-stop foraging. The FAO's Dr Cherukat Chandrasekharan estimated such non-wood values from world forests at $120 billion a year, but noted such users have no champion equal in power to clearcut loggers out to make a quick buck.[8]

Forests are a storehouse of snacks, treats and medicine. Forest honey has more anti-oxidants than field honey. Tree resin can make chewing gum, such as the chicle (whence Chiclets), which the ancient Mayans took from the sapodilla tree. Chewing gum made from trees is a $10 billion a year industry, according to the FAO's *Non-Wood News*.

Other treats come from 25,000 tonnes a year of Brazil nuts from the Amazonian rainforest, and 1,300 tonnes of pine nuts from the Kozac area of Turkey, where the forest is also used to graze cattle. Blueberries and raspberries are common in many woods, as are acai, the new berry hit from Brazil. Mushrooms and truffles have been rediscovered as gourmet-quality forest crops. For salad greens, try sorrel and spring leaves of willow. For Canada's wild spring green, try steaming fiddleheads. Forests also provide foods with medicinal properties, probably because deep-rooted trees raise scarce minerals to the surface. Ginseng

Food sovereignty

comes from the forest. So does yerba mate, the earthy but mineral-packed tea from the Amazon. So do boars and the original pigs. What the forest lacks in specialized crops, it makes up for in range of crops, one reason why indigenous and Southern food production almost always links food-medicine-fiber-fuel as one set of activities, commonly separated in a field culture.[9]

Forest favors
By making food security a walk in the woods, forest-based economies breed a spirituality that is gentler and more place-based and nature-worshiping than the jealous and competitive in-group religiosity that comes from drylands, cultural historian Brian Griffith has explained. Adds David Waltner-Toews, a leader of Veterinarians without Borders, forests nurture a sense that 'the nature of which we are a part is a kind of flexible, responsive, diverse welfare state'. Their views matched what I saw during a week in 2006 at the Sivinanda Yoga Ashram in the forested hilltown of Neyyar Dam in Kerala. The state is named after the coconut tree, which people use for 45 different purposes, from food to fuel to medicine to fiber. Typically, a canopy of tall rubber (used for surgical gloves) and coconut trees protects smaller fruit and spice trees below, all harvested on an ongoing basis by nearby townsfolk for food, fuel and medicines. The Ashram's massage therapist mixed his Ayurvedic ointments from roots and bark of various trees brought to a boil in coconut oil.[10]

In 2007, I met village leaders of two indigenous bands, the Apakararu and Pataxo, who live in northern Brazil. My colleague, Judy New, a nutritionist with Toronto's Indian Friendship Centre, immediately reached into her purse for her welcoming gifts, as they spontaneously reached for gifts to her. The only white

Anglo in the room, I sat on my hands with nothing to contribute, witness to two sharing cultures, separated by thousands of miles and as many years, but based on a common tradition of gift exchange, a commons-based strategy for gaining security through sharing rather than private savings.

The 'wild west' style takeover of Brazil's indigenous lands forced members of the two bands to relocate to an isolated and protected area in the north, where they are organizing their village around concentric circles of different foods. Manioc (cassava) will be grown close to their homes; further away will be bushes laden with berries and materials for crafts; yet further out will be trees for nuts, firewood and lumber, their leader, Toe, shows me. Manioc was first grown by Brazil's indigenous forest peoples, and features leaves and roots rich in protein, phosphorus, calcium and Vitamin C. The attention to food planning is obvious as they prepare to enter their village. Food is central to maintaining indigenous identity, says Geralda Soares, their researcher and translator. They eat common foods – manioc, melons, sweet potatoes, corn and fish. They work communally to prepare the fields, harvest the crops and celebrate their successes. 'Food is life. It is not just land, but culture, history and geography,' she says.

Forest ecosystems are under threat everywhere in the world but Europe, where forest cover increased from 989 to 1001 million hectares between 1990 and 2005. The European Union funded farmers who allowed forests to grow back over marginal farmlands, and the farmers responded, ending any mystery as to how reforestation can be made to happen quickly. The shift makes two contributions to reducing global warming emissions. It ends a negative: erosion of topsoil, which exposes soil carbon and releases carbon dioxide. It also starts a positive because growing trees act as a long-term 'sink', drawing down carbon from the atmosphere. Perhaps as forests grow in, farmers who come from a Northern culture that can't see the food for the trees will identify possibilities of finding a way to harvest food, not just carbon, from the forest.[11]

In Africa and South America, forest losses have been significant, threatening the forest food economy. Africa's forest cover declined from 699 to 635 million hectares between 1990 and 2005 while in South America coverage went from 891 to 832 million hectares. Asia and North America held steady. Unfortunately, my information only goes until 2005, and does not capture the devastation happening as complex forests are slashed across the Global South to make way for simplified plantations of palm to produce bio-fuels that will likely be marketed as 'green'.[12]

Meadow bounty

Meadows and wild grasslands harbor as many overlooked food, medicinal, fuel, fiber and fodder sources as forests. Some foods are wild plants and herbs which farmers (who call them weeds) want out of their fields. Many weeds are a nutritionist's field of dreams. Dandelions are a powerhouse of vitamins A and C, as well as minerals such as calcium, potassium, silicon and magnesium. Purslane, Gandhi's favorite vegetable, is rich in iron and vitamin C – a great combination against one of the most common and debilitating mineral deficiencies in the world – as well as omega 3 fatty acids. Stinging nettle is rich in B vitamins. Pigweed is a variant of amaranth, commonly recommended as ideal for fighting malnutrition. Wild groundnut tubers are high in protein and immune-building isoflavones.

'Mother Nature's grocery store,' one weed enthusiast claims.[13]

Like the forest, the open meadow is a buddy to people facing hard times. Leaves and stems of wild plants are tastiest in early spring salads, before domesticated greens have roused from their sleep. Dried seeds, nice in baked goods, are there in the late fall, after harvest is done. Wild plants are low-maintenance. Meadows are a no-till, no-GE, no-pesticide and fertilizer-free zone, which may account for their lack of promoters among farm input industries. The commons are a workshop for common people. They require few cash investments, respecting resources that are scarce. They do require labor and knowledge, resources that are plentiful. Government anti-poverty programs could well duplicate such empowering conditions.

Coastal delights

Ocean beaches offer another food and pharmaceutical commons, ideal for finding nutrient-rich greens, reds and browns, sometimes called seaweeds. I got a cook's tour of an ocean beach with marine biologist Irene Novaczek when I was volunteering on an organic farm in Prince Edward Island, on Canada's east coast in 2007.

As well as leading the Island Institute, which works with indigenous peoples in Chile to help them recover their healthy seaplant dietary traditions, Novaczek runs her own company, Oceanna Seaplants, which makes medicinal teas and creams from plants washed up on the beach. She introduced me to the intricacies of what experts call 'phycophagy' or 'marine algae', as she talked up her favorite sea vegetables – gracilaria, sugar kelp and wrack, all loaded with manganese, zinc and iodine, and all easy to slip into soups, salads or puddings.

Food sovereignty

The Cambridge World History of Food identifies sea plants as rich sources of protein, iodine, phenols, as well as essential fatty acids. More recently, a study in the *Journal of Nutrition* identified several varieties of seaweed as excellent sources of iron that the body can use easily. Seaplants were a central part of the human diet prior to the rise of agriculture, and continue to define many cuisines, most famously Japanese and Korean cuisines, which feature seaplants in salads, broths and wrapped around sushi. Surprisingly, bay leaves, one of the most popular cooking herbs in the North, have a name that tells where they come from, I realized as I walked through bushes of them on my way to find seagreens in Prince Edward Island.[14]

As with all foods from the commons, seaplants are free to those who invest their time and effort, but depend on informal knowledge that is usually developed and shared among women, and passed on as mother and child work the beaches together. Such informal knowledge is vulnerable to extinction, which, Novaczek says, dramatizes the urgency of saving that knowledge, particularly among marginalized coastal and island peoples. 'We need to work with the natural resources at hand and live within our means,' she says.

Insect bites

Entomophagy is another way to work the commons for food, still popular in most of the world. Ants, termites, locusts, grasshoppers, crickets, beetles, caterpillars and moths are among some 2000 species of insects enjoyed as snacks and delicacies. According to the *Cambridge World History of Food*, sago grubs wrapped in banana leaves and roasted on an open fire are raved over in Papua New Guinea, while large queen leafcutter ants are a delicacy in Colombia, and bee brood and honeycomb wrapped in banana leaves are hot in Thailand. Insects even make it in high-end dining. Chef Jean-Georges Vongerichten is testing ant larvae salad for the first Mexican eatery in his exclusive global chain, *Time* magazine reports.

Ohio State University extension programs identify insects as micro-livestock. Insect ranchers will like the low feed-to-meat ratio of their new herd, about a third that of other livestock. Nutritionists will be bug-eyed. Caterpillars match beef, pork, and chicken in protein, show stronger on iron, zinc, niacin, thiamine and riboflavin, and win hands-down in ratings for low cholesterol and high essential fats.

In a 2004 report for the FAO, Paul Vantomme identifies insects as a 'forgotten food crop' for the poor and disadvantaged. In many African villages, he says, trees are planted strategically to attract insects for a two-month period when they're rearing their young, which makes for easy pickings – the insect equivalent of low-hanging fruit. As with sea plants, field greens and forest snacks, women and children do the work without any owners or managers over them. The marginalizing of these food sources by field or plantation agriculture is a study in the ways Northern land-use practices imposed huge opportunity costs by overlooking food sources outside their range of vision. We are what we don't eat.[15]

QUESTION 3: WHAT IS FOOD?
According to eminent naturalist Edward O Wilson, varying groups of humans have eaten some 7,000 species of plants. That is a fraction of Nature's smorgasbord, which offers 30,000 edible species. 'Modern agriculture is only a sliver of what it could

be,' Wilson writes in *The Diversity of Life.* 'Waiting in the wings are tens of thousands of unused plant species, many demonstrably superior to those in favor,' such as the delicious lulo fruit of Colombia and Ecuador, or the winged bean of New Guinea, a 'one species supermarket'. Given Wilson's view on the abundance of food choices provided by Nature, it is no surprise that he is a critic of the conventional view that hunger comes from lack of money. People do not die for lack of income, he shows, but lack of access to the wealth of the commons. There's the rub: many of the 7,000 species that humans have nibbled on, and most of the 23,000 species they overlook, live in that no-one's-land known as the commons, and therefore lack any commercial value for corporations.[16]

Many people in the South look upon the forest, beach or meadow commons as something akin to a part-time job: a place to work during free time on off-season or slow days. Among people who live close to the edge, the food income from such part-time work makes all the difference for survival. For that reason, food from the commons is often called 'survival food'. When people play the field to gather foods from the commons, they also gain access to a wide range of foods and nutrients they don't get from their day job, which usually centers on a small number of staple crops. That makes commons food crucial to health, not just survival. Because knowledge to work the commons comes from a folk culture created by women, the foods are also crucial for maintaining popular traditions and women's esteem. For people with a living tradition of the commons, asking 'What is food?' is tantamount to asking 'How do we survive as a community?'.

These physical and cultural survival issues are most

poignant in Africa, the continent most colonized by plants from other continents. Experts fear Africa faces a 'genetic meltdown', and risks losing 2,000 livestock breeds and plants uniquely adapted to the climatic challenges it faces. Since indigenous foods have no appeal in Northern markets, commercial growers don't bother saving them. The commons stand between these breeds and extinction.

Kenyan ethno-botanist Patrick Maundu campaigns to save the food birthright of 'African spinach', hundreds of varieties of green leaves – many snipped from the commons in the 'cut and come again' tradition that allows repeated harvests from the same plants. Jeopardizing the future of this spinach undermines both nutrition and the crucial role of women gatherers, he says.[17]

Weedy politics

In India and Bangladesh, the link between access to the commons and support for health has produced a comprehensive rethink of food policy. Supporters of the New Agricultural Movement based in the floodplains of Bangladesh, and of the Deccan Development Society based in the dry plateau of southern India, say the issue is 'the politics of weeds'. In 2007, Farhad Mazhar and three colleagues wrote a report on weeds that poses changes to the ways agricultural, social, environmental, economic and spiritual issues are linked. The report, published in association with the International Development Research Centre in Canada, is called *Food Sovereignty and Uncultivated Biodiversity in South Asia: Essays on the Poverty of Food Policy and the Wealth of the Social Landscape*.[18]

They describe approximately 100 'uncultivated foods' that nourish people and livestock. Poor women take leaves from pumpkins and gourds in farmed fields, and leaves from other plants that are found beside laneways or around fences – wherever an orphaned patch of land is not owned by an individual, and has come to be accepted as public space. About 65 per cent of the food, fuel and fodder of poor villagers, and about 34 per cent of the needs of more affluent villagers, come from such spaces. Anti-poverty programs should be based on these successes, the Mazhar team says. 'In our view, the failure of poverty alleviation schemes is due to an overemphasis on income and employment initiatives and a profound disregard for expenditure-saving activities,' they argue.[19]

Since public access to the means of livelihood is crucial to everyone in a village, food sovereignty, or community control over local resources, is the question of the hour. Mazhar and his colleagues believe that three contributors to community control of food – biodiversity, local control and women-centered knowledge – are under threat by the WTO. These threats need to be countered by community rights to make food production 'a life-affirming practice and deeply human undertaking', they write. Likewise, food needs to be appreciated as more than a utility that staves off hunger. Food is 'a joy of life, produced and eaten not only to satisfy hunger, but also to savor and share with others in the community', they write. From such poor villages may come a future text on *The Abundance of Communities*, the food sovereignty response to Adam Smith's *The Wealth of Nations*.[20]

The life-sustaining heritage of the commons explains why food sovereignty grew out of the Global South during the late 1990s and early 2000s. A powerful new phrase in a field remarkably lacking in its own political terminology, food sovereignty resonates with the lived experience of ordinary people. It registers as a customary right that people can actually taste. East and west, north and south, social history shows that the most passionate rebellions of the most humble peoples have almost always come when customary rights seem in jeopardy. During the 1990s and early 2000s, when peasants in Asia and Africa worried that their well-being and community values were threatened by changes, they coined a phrase to express a right they hadn't thought about so deliberately before – food sovereignty, an umbrella necessary for the protection of food security and the individual right to food.

QUESTION 4: HOW DO WE GROW FOOD?
When it comes to food production methods, North is North, and South is South, and never the twain shall meet. I learned how true this is from Claudia Ho Lem in 2003, who told me about her work in the Philippines and China sponsored by a Southern-thinking Canadian organization called Resource Efficient Agricultural Production.

'It's no accident that agro-ecology comes out of the South,' says Ho Lem, an effervescent Canadian of mixed Polish, Chinese and First Nations descent. In the South, people need to entirely rethink crops and land-use left over from the colonial era, and recover the thinking that linked tropical climates, soils and plants before European colonizers came. To everything there is a season. Seasonal monsoons followed by seasonal dry spells in the South require as many unique food adaptations as seasonal cold and snow followed by hot summers require in the North. In this context, agro-ecology is the Southern how-to that goes with Southern community-specific food sovereignty.

Climate matters. When monsoon rains strike the

ground directly, the force is so powerful that it flushes out soil and nutrients, overloading water bodies with nutrients and killing the fish. Tropical forests adapted to this challenge by favoring tall trees with broad leaves that broke the rain's fall, under which stood shorter trees and bushes that let the water trickle down, thereby preventing erosion of nutrients needed by plants and harmful to fish.

Enter the Europeans, like bulls in a china shop, replacing diverse forest teamwork with one-crop plantation juggernauts of sugar cane, bananas and pineapple. These plants thrived in tropical warmth, but tropical soils during tropical storms didn't thrive with them – a classic example of shortsighted food planning.

To heal the colonial legacy, the Global South needs fundamental changes in land-use, crop choices and land-water relationships, Lo Hem tells me. That's where agro-ecology comes in. It features the Three Fs – food, fuel and fiber needed by the local community – so it has a wider palette of options than if heat-loving foods for export were the only consideration. The goal of local self-reliance, unlike the dictates of an import-export economy, mean local peasants and consumers can support multi-tasking on the three Fs needed to maintain balance in a sustainable tropical system. The How of doing food in different parts of the world requires many adaptations with varying internal trade-offs of efficiencies, not one universal dogma that assumes world growing conditions are uniform. The world is not flat, which is why food sovereignty is a precondition for harmonizing diversity with equality.

Goan for it

I saw another element of North-South difference when I arrived in Goa, India in December 2006. The day we arrived in this normally quiet, conservative, tourist-oriented state, there was a mass demonstration against Babush (a first name with letters that stand for bold, achieving, brilliant, understanding, simple and humble, his admirers said in a newspaper ad) Monserrate, the senior politician pushing freewheeling real-estate deals with resorts in the area – often by selling lands long occupied by tenant farmers, who were promptly sent packing. Daily protests continued for a week, the sense of community betrayal growing each day. 'If these atrocities continue, then the whole village will burn down the project,' one protester said. The brilliant but humble one had to step down from his high office.

Looking for a way to explain this level of popular militancy, I picked up a book called *The Goan Village Communes*. It turns out that the local people have run their farms as a village commune since 400 BCE. Despite Northern stereotypes of easy tropical living, weather extremes require co-operative effort. Villagers joined together to build structures that stored monsoon rainfall for later use in irrigation. According to Olivinho Gomes, the local author of the study, this village commune tradition was the 'bedrock of the Goan identity', that always rebelled against 'pernicious politicians who have transformed themselves into downright mercenary interests' to sell out community rights to determine land-use rules to benefit everyone. That precise tradition was revived in 2007, confirming the social historians' adage that positive collective experiences and memories must predate sudden exploitation for successful mass protests to develop. Treating land as a commodity didn't fit with how food systems needed to be developed in a Southern climate.[21]

I suspect that something similar was happening at the same time in West Bengal, where a self-described

Food sovereignty

Communist government was taking over farmland to gift it for a Tata Motors car factory. Dissident politician Mamata Banerjee launched a 25-day hunger strike to protest this confiscation of farmland, and gained national publicity. Whether it's for tourist facilities or factories, someone can always pay more money for land than farmers, so without powerful values that place farmland on a community pedestal, near-urban farmland is always at risk. This is the real (as in real estate) reason why community food security and food sovereignty are moving to the forefront of the discussion about the future of food, and challenging the concept that the food Why is primarily about economics. If food and farming are primarily business decisions, not community survival decisions, there is no farming future on any land that has another urban or industrial use. Food value does not rest on its commodity status, but its use value; that needs to become the foundation of food policy. Southern realities bring this aspect of food sovereignty and community food security down to earth.[22]

Peasant lands

I remember Hugo Blanco from the 1960s, when his fierce portrait under the slogan 'Land or Death' gained him an international reputation as a heroic fighter for Peruvian peasants struggling for land. In 1963, Blanco was sentenced to death for organizing a peasant land seizure, but the international campaign won his freedom. When I heard he'd come to Toronto in 2007, I had to meet this fiery revolutionist. He looked out at his audience with a toothy grin beaming from beneath a floppy sheepskin hat, the kind worn by the Quechua indigenous people of the frigid mountains of southern Peru. (I only learned afterward that he wears the hat on doctor's orders, for fear that a skull which has suffered too many police beatings can't take any accidental bumps now).

Even though he looks like a huggable grandpa, Blanco's opening line took me by surprise. Indigenous politics in South America (what he calls 'Abya Yala') are charged today, 500 long years after Europeans invaded, he says, because mining, oil and gas corporations have finally crossed the line. 'They are poisoning Pachamama, Mother Earth,' he says, and their greed threatens 'ayllu', the indigenous sense of community that includes every being in the village, including hills, rivers, animals, plants and vegetables, each endowed with one or more spirits. The combined destruction of Nature and community strike 'aggressively against the two chords of our culture,' he said, which the people must defend or lose forever.

I am struggling to break free from European ideas that remain stuck in my head, and to recover my indigenous identity, Blanco says. I'm still a socialist, he adds, but in an indigenous Peruvian, not a European, way. After all, reports of Inca civilization inspired Voltaire and Thomas More, contributing to Europe's tradition of utopian socialism. One of Blanco's daughters, herself raised in Sweden during one of his many exiles, led Swedish tourists through a Peruvian village and was told that it looked like socialism. You have that backwards, he recalls her telling the Swedes; socialism looks like this. Blanco has also localized his views about power. 'Among revolutionaries, we were negatively affected by obsession with power,' he says, but now, in keeping with indigenous traditions, 'we are not about taking power, but building power from below.' He likes to organize 'peasant circles', which displace judges and corrupt government officials with self-managing groups.

Indigenous roots

After the talk, I tuck into a two-hour dinner with Blanco, Phil Cournoyer, the translator of his memoirs, and assorted friends at a nearby internet café serving Somali food. Blanco is struggling to reconcile his earlier European-style radicalism with the rediscovery of his indigenous roots that South American governments have done their best to 'disappear', Cournoyer tells me. But when Blanco chanted Land or Death, he already had 'an incipient understanding' that he was saying something different from the popular Cuban cry, Fatherland or Death, Cornoyer says. As an indigenous person, he felt that land was linked to identity, meaning and life, not just a nation-state in struggle against an empire. Blanco, who is hungry and tired, interrupts. 'It is not the earth that belongs to the people, but the people who belong to the earth,' he says. From the leader of militant land reform during the 1960s comes a new land reform philosophy for the 21st century that comes out of the Global South traditions that spawned food sovereignty.

At 72, Blanco remains active as editor of *La Lucha Indigena* (the Indigenous Struggle) and leading spokesperson for the Peruvian peasants' union. Blanco's magazine immediately published the entire text of the Cochabamba Declaration, adopted by an indigenous conference in Bolivia on 12 October 2007, which celebrated the UN adoption of a declaration of rights for the world's 370 million indigenous peoples, most of whom live in the Global South. The declaration hails a new 'millennium of life, of balance, and wholeness, without having to abuse energies that destroy Mother Earth', and calls on governments to 'implement national policies for food sovereignty as the main basis of national sovereignty in which the community guarantees both respect for its own culture and its places and ways of carrying our production, distribution and consumption in harmony with the nature of healthy, uncontaminated food available to all, eliminating hunger because alimentation is a life right.' 12 October was proclaimed 'Beginning Day of our Struggles to Save Mother Nature.'[23]

Until the 1990s, one of the turning-point decades of modern history, traditional village patterns survived, met personal needs and fulfilled community functions, protected to some extent by isolation and benign neglect. No longer protected by the benign neglect of isolation after the 1990s, searching for new ways to defend local wealth and traditions for the future, community members turned a set of communal traditions, spiritual beliefs, and ways of partnering with the land into a platform – food sovereignty.

1 L McQuaig, *The Cult of Impotence: Selling the Myth of Powerlessness in the Global Economy* (Penguin Canada, 1999). **2** World Bank, *World Development Report, 2008, Agriculture for Development (World Bank, 2007)*; 'Two Myths that Keep the World Poor,' *Ecologist*, July-August 2005. **3** G Kent, 'Fish Trade, Food Security, and the Human Right to Adequate Food,' in *FAO Fisheries report No. 708 FIIU/R708*, Report of the Expert Consultation on International Fish Trade and Food Security, Casablanca, (FAO, 2003). **4** S Nolen, 'How Malawi went from a nation of famine to a nation of feast,' in *Globe and Mail*, 12 October 2007; www.theglobeandmail.com/servlet/story/RTGAM.20071012.food12/ BNStory/International/home ; *New York Times*. Celia Dugger, 'Ending Famine, Simply by Ignoring the Experts,' in *New York Times*, 2 December 2007. www.nytimes.com/2007/12/02/world/africa/02malawi.html?_ r=1&oref=slogin&ref. **5** See W Roberts et al., *Real Food For a Change* (Random House, 1999) pp.107-11; D Marino, 'Water and Food Safety in the Developing World: Global Implications for Health and Nutrition of Infants and Young Children' in *Journal of the American Dietetic Association*, November, 2007. **6** www.parentnetsweden.com/Infopages/Resources/ Home_Garden_directory/koloni.htm or www.koloni.org **7** 'Deforestation, Climate Change Magnify East African Drought,' at www.ens-newswire. com/ens/jan2006/2006-01-16-02.asp; United Nations Environment

Food sovereignty

Program, GEO4 (Progress Press, 2007) p.100. **8** *Non-Wood News*, July, 2007. **9** See generally, the FAO publication, *Non-Wood News*, and the Community Forestry Resource Centre, both accessible online. **10** Brian Griffith, *The Gardens of Their Dreams: Desertification and Culture in World History* (Fernwood, 2001); D. Waltner-Toews, *The Chickens Fight Back: Pandemic Panics, and Deadly Diseases that Jump from Animals to Humans* (Greystone, 2007) p.60. **11** Doug Saunders, 'The hush-hush regreening of Europe,' Toronto *Globe and Mail*, 2 December, 2007 – www.globeandmail.com/servlet/story/RTGAM.20071220.wreckondoug1221/BNStory/International/?pageRequested+2 **12** 'Forest Cover Indicator 1990-2005,' at Earth Policy Institute, www.earthpolicy.org **13** W Roberts, *Get A Life!* (Toronto, 1995), T Dean, 'Stalking the Wild Groundnut,' *Orion Magazine*, November-December, 2007; see Steve Brill website www.wildmanstevebrill.com **14** Food Navigator.com 23 November 2007, citing research in *Journal of Nutrition*, December, 2007; for sources and intricacies of seaplants, see W Roberts, 'Fishsticks these ain't,' *This Magazine*, November-December, 2007. www.thismagazine.ca/issues/2007/11/fishticks.php **15** For sources and more examples, see W Roberts, 'Eating Insects: Waiter, there's no fly in my soup,' *Alternatives Journal*, January 2008. **16** EO Wilson, *The Diversity of Life* (Harvard University Press, 1992) pp 287-9. **17** BBC posting, on listserv, soilandhealth 4 September 2007; Environmental News Service, 3 September 2007; Common Dreams, 5 September 2007; FAO, 'The State of the World's Animal Genetic Resources,' posted on FoodNews 12 September 2007; http://allafrica.com/stories/200709070697.html and www.futureharvest.org/pdf/leafy_feature.shtml **18** F Mazhar, *Food Sovereignty and Uncultivated Biodiversity in South Asia* (Academic Foundation, 2007); and at www.irdc.ca/openbooks/337-9. see also Greenpeace, Bread for the World, 'recipes against hunger: success stories for the future of agriculture' September 2001. **19** *Food Sovereignty and Uncultivated Biodiversity*, p 56. **20** Ibid, p 10. **21** Mumbai, *Indian Express*, 19 December 2006, *Panjim Herald*, 20 December 2006, *Gomantak Times*, 23 December 2006; OJ Gomes, *The Goan Village Communes*, (Vasantrao Dempo Education and Research Foundation, 2005). **22** *Navind Times*, 25 December 2006, Mumbai *Hindustan Times*, 27 December 2006, India News Online, 1 January 2007. **23** 'Indigenous Peoples of South America Adoption of UN Declaration on the Rights of Indigenous Peoples,' translated by P Cornoyer, posted FoodNews 6 October 2007.

4 Bread and roses

Whether it is caused by lack of money or sheer lack of food, hunger can be overcome when governments empower citizens. When we understand this, we see the reason for advances in Brazil and Cuba, progress that can be made elsewhere.

I WAS EASY enough to spot: a balding Anglo standing on the steps of Havana's Capitol Building, carrying 30 meters of watering hose, a donation to a children's garden that my host Roberto asked me to bring from Canada – a good introduction to his resourcefulness, as well as the equipment shortages Cubans endure as they try to feed themselves from city gardens. But I had no idea how to spot Roberto Perez Rivero, the informal ambassador for urban agriculture in Cuba and one of the leading spokespersons for Cuba's respected Foundation for Nature and Man. No problem. Wearing shorts and a T-shirt, looking a bit sunburned, he waved at me from 10 meters away. I decided to take the day off and go to the beach, he said, pointing to his clothes, and off we went to an out-of-the-way Havana restaurant that specialized in Cuban-style Chinese fare. We were good buddies by the end of dinner.

Perez Rivero's organization was launched in 1994, when the worst of what Cubans know as the 'special period' – a time of painful adjustment to the collapse of Cuba's ally, the Soviet Union, the equivalent to their own economic floor falling out from under them – was just about over. The formation of his non-governmental organization was part of what Perez Rivero calls an 'NGO boom' during the mid-1990s, when young activists formed some 3,000 organizations to raise money from international donors to fund their pioneering work. While the special period was bottoming out, without Russian oil or grains to feed Cuba's people and machines, and without Soviet purchases of

Bread and roses

Cuban sugar and oranges to finance buying food and other basics, the typical Cuban went hungry. Food intake fell by almost a third, from an average of 2,900 calories per person each day during the 1980s to 1,863 calories in 1994, well below the recommended amount for a healthy and active life.

But these hard times were also the time of Cuba's 'glasnost', of being open to learn and change. The Government was encouraging independent organizations like Perez Rivero's, and giving them leeway to explore frontier ideas. A government that believed in state ownership helped the unemployed become self-employed garden entrepreneurs, selling what they grew on public lands at farmers' markets. Cuba had long taken pride in its old-line style of Communism, unflinching toward Yankee imperialism. But it had been equally unbending in loyalty to 1950s Modernist ideals of high-tech, high-input farming in state-run and worker collectives. To give the green light to independent NGOs and small entrepreneurs was a major shift in government policy and a sea change in approaches to food and agriculture.

Cuban 'glasnost'

Perez Rivero is a creation of this Cuban glasnost. In his twenties during the hardest times of the special period, he sowed his political wild oats during a Renaissance of experimentation, bold actions and ideas. I grew up thinking there were three choices in the world, he told me: a society controlled by the market, a society controlled by the state, or one where community groups were in control. To test the waters, he founded a magazine called 'It's possible', a title that sums up his approach to urban agriculture and green community economic development.

Holding firm to its egalitarian principles, the Cuban Government shared the burden of hard times evenly, by rationing food and other necessities, and strictly limiting expenditures on luxuries that could eat up resources for crucial needs. Daily rations were basic and frugal: beans, peas, rice, a little meat, quite a bit of sugar, no fruits or veggies, and no treats. Some of the cuts to luxuries really hurt, especially one limiting funerals to three bouquets of flowers. Community gardeners saw the business opportunity, and started growing flowers. They were in a grand proletarian tradition, launched by two teenage girls on strike against a New Jersey textile factory shortly before World War One. On the picket line, the girls carried a placard with their own hand-written message that became a global symbol of how horizons of hope grow when people in poverty move forward in a common cause: 'We want bread and we want roses'. Community gardeners, key to Cuba's success overcoming food insufficiency that might have condemned many to severe hunger, have long taken time to enjoy the flowers.

This chapter looks at Cuba's campaign against hunger, which is special because it coincided with drastic declines in the availability of fossil-fuel energy for the machines that helped produce food and the trucks that brought food to cities. Whether the coincidence of two shortages made success easier or harder is also a mystery to be explored. The chapter will then review Brazil's very different, but also quite successful, campaign against hunger.

Hunger's many facets

These two landmark cases of vigorous campaigns against hunger can help assess two powerful views about the abject failure of other governments to confront hunger's causes. One view comes from Amartya Sen, who won the Nobel Prize in economics for his studies on the economics of famines. Famines are not caused by lack of food, Sen argues, but lack of rights. When people blame famines on food shortages caused by natural disasters, they miss the real problem: a social disaster caused by a shortage of rights. 'Hunger is a many-headed monster,' he and his colleague Jean Druze write, so people suffering from hunger likely suffer from a disempowering combination of racism, sexism, prolonged poverty, illiteracy, lack of health-care, water, jobs, and above all lack of money with which to buy food. Confront these, and managing famine becomes a piece of cake, they suggest: 'So easy to prevent that it is amazing that they are allowed to occur at all.' Sometimes famine prevention is as easy as sponsoring public works programs that pay members of at-risk groups so they can buy the food they need from nearby farmers. Both the Cuban and Brazilian experience speak to this provocative analysis.[1]

Jacques Diouf of the UN Food and Agriculture Organization also writes frequently and eloquently about the need to win the race against hunger, as he urges in the preface to the FAO's 2006 annual report. He agrees that hunger is not a problem caused by shortage of food. 'What is lacking is sufficient political will to mobilize these resources to the benefit of the hungry,' he says. 'It can be done.' Both the Cuban and Brazilian cases allow us to unpack what 'political will' might mean and how it comes into the food picture.[2]

Cuban garden revolution

Cuba's campaign to prevent hunger is closely linked to its campaigns to promote urban and organic agriculture. Three factors probably account for the prominence of city gardens and organic growing meth-ods in an anti-hunger strategy. First, Cuba has long been a highly urbanized country. Most of the people who need food live in the city.

Second, Cuba had a food problem because it had a fuel shortage. Its agricultural practices were almost as mechanized and fertilizer-dependent – another way of saying oil-dependent – as those of the US. The easiest starting place to solve a food-related energy problem is in the city. Most obviously, city farms eliminate the need to transport food to the city, and to keep the food chilled during its commute so it doesn't go bad. If city people can walk down the road to buy fresh produce every day, they don't need packaging, a big fridge or any of the other energy hogs of a conventional food system. Less obviously, farming in the city provides access to urban waste that can substitute for farm inputs. Think compost, which overruns most cities with what is foolishly classed as a waste, rather than a misplaced resource. Compost can help displace fertilizers based on fossil fuels at the same time as it eliminates the need for fossil fuel in garbage pick-up and hauling – a double win for energy savings.

Third, cities are ideal for production of the very foods that should be the mainstay of the diet of (mostly sedentary) city people – veggies and fruit. Rural areas are better at producing grains, carbs and meat, which need lots of low-cost growing space. Cuba's rural farms, a legacy of slavery and colonialism, were often for sugar and tobacco, but rarely for fruits and vegetables, which were mostly imported before the 1990s.

Perez Rivero describes the traditional Cuban diet as 'redundant in carbohydrates', as in white rice, sugar and sugared drinks. Before the 'special period', obesity rates in Cuba ran at 30 per cent, then fell to 16 per cent as a result of food deprivation. Someone may have seen city farming as an opportunity to wean Cubans off empty calorie-dense carbs, and onto nutrient-dense, calorie-light fruits and vegetables. The Government actually shut down sugar mills with 400,000 hectares in sugar plantations and redirected those lands toward food production. But the switch to greens took a lot of sweet talk. Perez Rivero remembers that many early gardeners put down greens as weeds and rabbit food. His organization helped put on courses about nutrition as well as cooking classes.

Bread and roses

The output of vegetables from city farms tripled during the 1990s, and city farms now grow enough to meet the minimal nutrition needs of the population. City farms not only moved food closer to the people; it moved people closer to food and food further towards nutrition and energy-light organic gardening methods. Some forget that the purpose of Cuba's agricultural revolution was to end hunger in the face of energy shortage, and think the success story that has to be studied is the unprecedented conversion of a food system toward low-energy organic methods. All four elements – city location, organic (low energy) methods, nutritious foods and hunger prevention – evolved as an integrated whole.

Gardens for all

National and city governments seemed to favor letting a thousand veggies bloom when it came to different types of city farms. Some city plots were designed for people who lost their jobs and checked out gardening as a career. Other plots, often on the grounds of hospitals, schools and workplaces, provide food for staff and clients. Still others provide neighborhoods, while others produce for farmers' markets. All told, gardens take up about 12 per cent of Havana's space.

Perez Rivero provides training for people working small lots to supply an immediate neighborhood, part of a plan to have one plot for every 15 housing units. He takes me to a small home in a low-income area. Behind the house at ground level are several piles of truck tires that have been filled with composted soil and converted into planters. An old bathtub is another container. The more containers, the merrier the intensive gardening; plants can grow higher, and they can droop, allowing containers to double the production in small places. Overhead are two roof gardens loaded with tires and pots. I spot papaya, guava, onions, spinach, grapes (one roof is given over to them alone), basil, oregano, pomegranate, sweet pepper, aloe, tomatoes, and what Perez tells me is a 'nani tree, the fruit of the future'. He expects the three six- by six-meter gardens here can contribute significantly for five families. In case of funerals or weddings, there are also flowers.

Cuba's first success was to overcome the severe shortages of the special period. The next phase will be to move from embracing the necessity (the lack of fuel) to embracing the virtues – opportunities to promote nutrition, organic methods and green community economies. There are many reasons why Cubans came this far, and are prepared to go further. They are well educated, which makes it easier to learn and adapt. The State can mobilize resources to make sure things get done, such as delivery of free or low-cost meals to all childcare centers, schools, and large workplaces, which guarantees most people at least one nutritious meal every day. Though not a democracy, the Cuban Government can work with people to empower them. There are 67 extension agents in Havana to advise growers, for example, and 220 crop protection institutes to advise people on green-friendly sprays. The creation of a popular revolution, Cuba is also peppered with grassroots groups of many kinds, including unions, women's groups and multi-purpose Committees in Defense of the Revolution. 'Some organizations can snap their fingers and bring a million people out on a mobilization,' says Perez Rivero. Without these collective institutions, and without this institutional capacity of both government and civil society, Cuba could still be in its special period or worse. Anti-hunger advocates need to see nurturing such an institutional culture as part of their work.

It's almost 20 years since Cuba entered its special period, and it's not special any more. That makes Perez Rivero happy. 'We need to get rid of the label that this is because of an emergency,' he says. Crisis led them to the multiple benefits of doing some pivotal things right. So collecting food scraps and containers for urban gardens isn't just for hard times. 'If we manage garbage properly, we get rid of rats, we get rid of garbage trucks and their fumes and noise, we get plants that pump oxygen into the air, we get plants that store carbon and fix nitrogen.' Perez Rivero is referring to the 'cascade effect', which is central to food planning design. Like a cascade of water down a cliff, the benefits of food initiatives continue to flow into an ever-widening range of territory. Start with a garden project to improve nutrition, then watch the benefits of exercise, socializing with neighbors, knowledge about environmental processes, reduction in greenhouse gases, increased safety in parks, improvements in the walkability of cities, enhanced entrepreneurial skills, heightened interest of tourists ... and on and on; which is how we get to bread and roses too.[3]

Brazilian Zero Hunger

The language of Cuba is Spanish, and that of Brazil is Portuguese. But that's not the reason their food talk is different. People in Brazil's *Zero Fome* (Zero Hunger) movement use very different words from people working with Cuba's gardening revolution. Empowerment, inclusion, ethics, citizenship, civil society, base organization, capacity building, rights, duties – these are words that crop up when the campaign, launched in 2004, is discussed. More ambitious than the reduction-by-half goal set by the UN, Brazil's campaign strives to free almost 40 million people, a fifth of the population, from hunger by the end of the decade.

I and four other Torontonians are among a small group of foreigners invited to the campaign launch, an expression of thanks to our city for offering refuge to Herbert (Betinho) de Sousa during the 1970s, after he was exiled by military dictators in both Chile and his native Brazil. De Sousa returned to Brazil and led a campaign that is credited with inspiring the Lula Government's Zero Hunger commitment. People such as de Sousa helped Brazilians develop new words and ethics around hunger that are signposts of the intellectual and emotional distance traveled since 1950s Modernism, the impact of which is overpowering in the capital city of Brasilia, built from scratch at the height of Modernist brutalism. Barely a word is heard from President Lula about efficiency, production, feeding the world, compost, community or even agriculture during the 2004 conference. Instead, empowerment is on everyone's lips.

'I never used the word empowerment before 1997,' my traveling companion Debbie Field tells me, as we take a cab to the conference center named after de Sousa and an earlier anti-hunger crusader. Field opens a photo album, and shows me pictures of women she met during a 1997 trip to Brazil. The women had just built their homes with bricks they made in a hand-operated machine that de Sousa bought with donations from a nearby synagogue. 'He believed in us, so we believed in ourselves, and look what we did for ourselves,' the women told Field.

'That was Betinho's gift,' Field told me. He got people proud enough to 'do things for themselves, without waiting for government to get its act together, but still seeing the need for government action'. Betinho taught Torontonians and Brazilians that 'social movements should be about ethics, solidarity, transparency and citizenship' and that 'citizenship is a two-way street, not just about government doing things for people,' Field said.

Suddenly, the cab driver stops the car, turns around, and grabs Field's arms. 'You knew Betinho!' he shrieked. 'You knew Betinho!' Betinho, means 'little guy', a reference to his being short and slight. By this name is he loved and cherished many years after his death. 'This tiny man with giant charisma lifted a nation's hopes, and became the collective metaphor of an aroused Brazilian democracy,' is how one of his first Toronto friends, Judy Hellman, puts it.

When the Brazilian dictatorship stepped down in 1979, Betinho came home. He quickly organized IBASE (the Brazilian Institute for Social and Economic Analysis), one of the first independent organizations in democratic Brazil. A hemophiliac, he contracted AIDS from a blood transfusion in 1985. In 1986, he founded one of the world's premier organizations confronting AIDS. In 1993, he started Citizens Action against Hunger and Poverty and For Life. Its slogan was 'Hunger Can't Wait'. The organization quickly won backing from a thousand civil-society organizations, and set up 5,000 action committees. To speed up implementation, Betinho launched the Committee of Public Enterprises to Fight Hunger. In 1993, it enlisted 33 public firms and universities to donate surplus materials to create hundreds of brick-making machines, fish farms, urban gardens, and to become customers of newly formed worker co-ops.

'A rich diversity of direct, local, self-help, independent and grassroots engagement comes from the bottom-up nature of social movements in Brazil,' says Jaime Kirzner-Roberts, a Latin American specialist at Princeton University. 'It's a gut reaction and article of faith among those who've suffered so long from the concentration of power around a tiny economic and government élite,' she says. Popular organizations in Brazil, much quicker than their counterparts in North America and Europe, learned to spread their wings and extend their power base beyond the state, she says.

A beautiful horizon

Belo Horizonte, an industrial city that's home to about three million people – with over one million people, including 38 per cent of children, living below the poverty line – is a success story of municipal human rights-based programs against hunger. Since Patrus Ananias of the Workers' Party won the mayoralty in 1993, hunger levels have gone down. The center of the action is the city's Secretariat of Supplies, because Mayor Ananias wanted the lead department to focus on delivering the goods. All people have a right to adequate amounts of quality food, he said, and 'it is the duty of governments to guarantee this right'.

Compare the Mayor's focus on supply provision with what the UN expects from national governments. In 1999, the UN adopted General Comment 12, a helpful guide to categories of action that national governments can follow to honor food obligations. The list starts with respect, upholding the access people already have – respecting gardening as a legitimate function of green space in cities, for example. The list moves on to protect, using government powers to keep anyone from taking away existing access to food – not allowing a beach hotel to stop villagers from fishing off a beach, for example. The list proceeds to fulfill, part 1, facilitating access to food – organizing community gardens, for example. The list ends with fulfill, part 2, actually providing food to people in dire need – after a hurricane or flood, for example.[4]

When I was working on Toronto's food and hunger action plan, we came up with a similar grid, adapted to the capabilities of a Northern city government. Start with advocate: the mayor can pressure a senior level of government to improve school meals, for instance. Move on to co-ordinate: city staff can help citizens organize a farmers' market at City Hall, for example. Carry on with support: city staff can offer park space and equipment to help a neighborhood group start a community garden, for example. Then innovate: adopt incentives for green roofs where food can be grown, for example. Both the United Nations and the City of Toronto guidelines avoided a showdown on big budget items that come with direct provision of food to people who are hungry. Both guidelines respond to the pressure of what's called the 'neoliberal' approach to government that has held sway internationally since the 1990s: government's job is to steer the boat, not row the boat, the mantra goes.

Ananias, by contrast, set out to rock the boat by starting with three 'lines of action', all of which required direct government provision. That puts Belo Horizonte way out in front of what's expected, even from progressive governments.[5]

Belo started with a 'first line of action' aimed at people suffering malnutrition. One program supplied nutrient-rich 'flour' – made of wheat flour, corn flour, wheat bran, ground egg shells and powder from manioc leaves – for pregnant women and nursing moms. More recently, meals for children at schools or in city-run childcare centers qualified as first-line assistance. The city's sanitation department picks up unsold food at farmers' markets at the end of a day, then cleans and vacuum-packs it for delivery to neighborhood organizations serving members on low income. A city-sponsored food bank does the same with donations from supermarkets.

The 'second line of action' helps businesses respond to the needs of people on low incomes. Two medium-sized 'popular restaurants' are supported by the city. They are open for lunch and dinner on workdays. Meals are simple but nutritious. Rice, beans, salad and fruit are typical. All customers pay the same subsidized rate. Customers include workers, students, homeless youth, street vendors and seniors. Regulars join an organization that lobbies for improvements. Also on the list for second line of action are 4,000 modestly subsidized 'popular food baskets', with about 20 food basics. A list of prices at stores across the city is widely posted, helping people on low incomes use their food dollars well.

A 'third line of action' works on 'incentives to basic

food production'. One program helps local farmers bring fresh produce to the city. This is a four-way win for food security. It raises the incomes of small farmers, helping them overcome hunger. It helps small farmers stay on the land instead of swelling the numbers of those desperate for city shelter and jobs. It increases the availability of nutritious foods, since large farms in Brazil are typically dedicated to the export of sugar and oilseeds, leaving small farmers to handle fruit and veggies for locals. Fourth, by increasing supply, the price of produce is kept stable. In another third line of action, the city orders local produce for 155,000 meals a day in popular restaurants and schools. City staff teach backyard gardening and artisanal food preparation to help residents become self-employed or self-sufficient. Little wonder that Belo Horizonte has the highest consumption of fruit and vegetables in Brazil.[6]

'Hunger cannot wait'

The Zero Hunger campaign is mainly a national campaign. President Lula of the Workers' Party helps lead that campaign, and serves as its figurehead, speaking passionately about his youth as a poor shoeshine boy who often went hungry. He repeats Betinho's slogan, 'hunger cannot wait' – an antidote to well-fed people who argue that money for anti-hunger programs can be found later, when other budget priorities are not so pressing.

National initiatives are well funded and smartly planned. 'Bolsa Familia', a family allowance program created in 2003, reached about 45 million people by 2007, a quarter of Brazil's population, at an annual cost of over $4 billion. The money goes directly from the national government to the bank accounts of families living in poverty, with no bureaucracy or expenses in between – an important point for Lula's party, which fears both bureaucratic inertia and corrupt or 'clientelist' relations between local powerbrokers and individuals in their patronage networks. Children in families receiving the allowance are required to attend school regularly, and children and pregnant or nursing moms are required to visit health clinics regularly, a shrewd way of turning a short-term anti-hunger program into a long-term public health program. Nationally funded school meals, often the main meal of the day for children in poor regions of the North and Northeast, are served to 36 million children. Food orders for school meals go to small farms, where 77 per cent of agrarian workers are employed. In another of his first-term programs, Lula spent close to $5 billion to settle over 350,000 of the country's four million landless farm families, many of them supporters of the militant Landless Workers' Movement, on idle farm parcels owned by rich landowners.[7]

In his second term, Lula moved into the second phase of his anti-poverty initiatives with a 'Territories of Citizenship' program, which will be rolled out with a $6.4 billion budget for 2008. Funds will be used to improve schools and clinics and to bring electricity to about 1,000 towns scattered over 60 areas of Brazil that have been identified by the UN as most at risk for poverty and ill-health. The program is astutely packaged as infrastructure development, designed to provide jobs and job training. Those with an eye to program design will note that members of Lula's Workers' Party are highly sensitive about the country's tradition of 'clientelism', which pauperized poor people by making them dependent for favors on members of the élite. Workers' Party programs therefore strive to deliver food through collective institutions (distribution of food bank food through neighborhood organizations, for example) or deliver assistance through employment, clinics or schools.[8]

Brazil's national initiatives, along with several of Belo Horizonte's local offerings, aim to match the assessment of Nobel economist Amartya Sen, who argued that inequity is the demon behind hunger. The Workers' Party strives to overcome hunger by confronting inequality, but has a long way to go. *The Economist* rated the country's income distribution in 2007 as the most egalitarian in 25 years; as a result, the poorer half of Brazilians increased their share of national income from 9.8 to 11.9 per cent between 2002 and 2006, while the share going to the wealthiest 10 per cent slipped from 49.5 to 47.1 per cent. Nor has the Workers' Party challenged the dominant food system, which remains under the control of exporters of soy (for livestock) and sugar.[9]

Food availability

Inequity in social relations, at least within one country, played less of a role in Cuba's anti-hunger initiatives, perhaps because the deepest inequities were removed in the early years of the Cuban revolution, when the rich fled to the US. A general level of equality doubtless made it easier for Cuba to confront the production problems it had to overcome. That's a major reason why Cuba was able to organize food production and distribution on a community basis, rather than on the basis of income, as in Brazil. The depth of Cuba's problem with food availability, however, creates problems for Sen's analysis, which doesn't put much stock in the importance of actual food availability. Sen may need to update his analysis as Cuba-type scenarios become more common in a world of increasing climate chaos and resource scarcity. It may be that food availability issues will return to haunt human societies. It may even be that the future value of equity will be its ability to serve as a social resource that enables effective community and government action – a real reversal in the roles equity and hunger have played historically. The more egalitarian a society, we might suggest, the less plagued it will be by resentments, and the more

Heads we win, tails you lose

The two sides of the cheap food coin come from Engles' Law: the rich spend a smaller portion of a larger income on essentials. Low wages in food producing areas keep food proportionately more expensive. So rising food prices cause a hiccup in one area, pneumonia in another.

Cheap food is cheaper in some countries than others

Country	Food as % of Household Spending, 2006
United States	5.8
United Kingdom	8.7
France	13.9
Japan	14.3
South Africa	21.4
Chile	23.7
Mexico	24.5
India	33.4
Vietnam	39.7
Egypt	41.5
Azerbaijan	51.6

Adapted from USDA, ERS, Briefing Rooms, 'Food CPI, Prices and Expenditures: Expenditures on Food, by Selected Countries, 2006'

inclusive and resilient it will be as neighbors work to solve common problems. Any government plans to forestall possible supply shortage of the future should start dealing with equity, inclusion and resilience now.

The centrality of popular organizations in both Cuba and Brazil could be instructive for Jacques Diouf of the FAO. Brazil's and Cuba's successes confirm that hunger can be addressed by governments with modest resources; to that extent, action and victory are matters of political will. But political will comes from those who are aggrieved having 'agency' – being conscious about their problem, aware of alternatives, and capable of taking effective action. Brazil's leaders recognize this agency issue explicitly.

At the 2004 conference I attended, former Belo Mayor Ananias joined President Lula's cabinet as Minister for Social Development and Hunger Alleviation. Speaking to a thousand people at the Zero Hunger launch, he stressed that social justice and personal ethical development are 'the greatest goals we have' – a formulation that expresses the inspiration of Roman Catholic liberation theology among Brazilian food activists. We 'need to have popular democracy in place where citizens have rights and duties,' as well as 'social control over the state' and 'autonomy of social movements,' Ananias said, 'as in Belo Horizonte.' As with so much of the Brazilian anti-hunger liturgy, this formulation expresses a strong commitment to robust citizen organizations. Although Cuba lacks Brazil's open and competitive political democracy and media, it has more than its share of lively and dynamic organizations. Such 'communities of food practice', which share ideas, connections, good times and bad, are a precondition to effective food policy development, as sociologist Harriet Friedmann has shown. Political knowhow can be as important as political will. The centrality of such grassroots capacity is one reason why municipal governments, historically closest to community groups, need to be identified as crucial government actors in food security program planning.[10]

Most impressive to me, though overlooked by analysts such as Sen and Diouf, is the intuitive understanding Cuban and Brazilian leaders have for programs. 'Policy is for wonks, programs are for implementers' is an indelicate way to classify people who work on food and related issues. Policy has the prestige, but programmers get the job done. Brazil and Cuba, in sharp contrast to many jurisdictions, had the capacity and knack to develop programs with goals, deliverables, budget lines, staff, partnerships – the works. This is what puts food on the table. Belo Horizonte put its top priority food programs in the trust of the most humble department of a city, Supplies, because the mayor wanted to deliver to people who had rights. Such humility and such commitment to serve are pivotal to success.

1 A Sen, *Development and Freedom* (Random House, 1999) pages 162-180, J Druze and A Sen, *Hunger and Public Action* (Oxford, 2006). **2** FAO, *The State of Food Insecurity in the World 2006 Eradicating World Hunger – taking stock ten years after the World Food Summit* (FAO, 2006) p 4,7. **3** For two excellent references, see F Funes et al, *Sustainable Agriculture and Resistance: Transforming Food Production in Cuba* (Food First, 2002), M Cruz and R Medina, Agriculture in the City: A Key to Sustainability in Havana, Cuba (IDRC 2001). **4** United Nations, Economic and Social Council, Committee on Economic, Social and Cultural Rights, *General Comment 12*: Geneva: ECOSOC E/C.12/1999/5. **5** City of Toronto, Food and Hunger Action Committee, *Planting the Seeds* (2000) and *The Growing Season* (2001). **6** Cecilia Rocha, 'Urban Food Security Policy: The Case of Belo Horizonte, Brazil,' *Journal for the Study of Food and Society*, 5, 1, Summer 2001, pp36-47; C Rocha and Adriana Aranha, 'Urban Food Policies and Rural Sustainability – How the Municipal Government of Belo Horizonte, Brazil is promoting Rural Sustainability' unpublished paper. **7** C Rocha, 'Update from Brazil: Advancing food and nutrition security under the Lula government,' presentation to Canadian Association of Food Studies annual conference, Saskatoon, 2007; J Pedro Stedile, 'The Class Struggle in Brazil: The Perspective of the MST,' *Socialist Register*, 2008, L Panitch and C Leys, eds., *Socialist Register: Global Flashpoints: Reactions to Imperialism and Neoliberalism* (Merlin Ross, 2008). **8** 'Brazil unveils anti-poverty drive,' *BBC News*, 26 February 2008, 'Brazil unveils $6.4 billion poverty plan,' *International Herald Tribune*, 25 February 2008. **9** M Osava, 'Brazil: No Consensus on Success of Land Reform,' *Inter Press Service News Agency*, 22 March 2007; *The Economist*, 'Dreaming of glory: a special report on Brazil,' 14 April 2007, pp 12, 14. **10** H Friedmann, 'Scaling up: Bringing public institutions and food service corporations into the project for a local, sustainable food system in Ontario,' in *Agriculture and Human Values*, 24:3, 2007.

5 Gluttons for punishment

The rise of cheap food, the decline of Northern manufacturing and the fall of Southern 'development' during the 1970s were all part of the same puzzle. When we understand that, we learn that a lot more than bad diets came from the rise of junk food.

I SAW THE light on abundance at seven o'clock on a sunny August morning on my first day back volunteering at Stowel Lake Farm on Saltspring Island, a little piece of paradise on Canada's west coast. It was my second season, so I knew the breakfast routine. I walked about 30 meters from our cabin and started picking from a wild patch of juicy blackberries. I picked two cereal bowls of berries while standing in one place, thanks to a little trick for seeing more than meets the eye. Gently bobbing the branches, I could see berries formerly lurking in the shadows, as plump and juicy as any. Just looking beyond what stared me in the face doubled the berries from one spot. I bobbed the bush again, and bouncing shadows brought more berries into view, no longer hidden by the blinding glare. There should be a parable of the right mix of light, shadow and angle for berry picking, I thought. Abundance is all around us; we just have to look for it in the right light.

Later that same day, I learned the awful truth about blackberry bounty when I went into town and saw the August 2006 edition of the regional farm paper, *Country Life*. I suddenly saw the wealth of perfect berries through the eyes of commercial growers. The front-page story said berry producers across the Pacific Northwest expected their worst season in 15 years – unless a cold snap or heat wave finished off Serbian berries. Otherwise, markets glutted by Serbian berries would destroy the price of fresh and local berries from two continents, one ocean and thousands of kilometers away. In the eyes of farmers facing global rivals, nature's bounty is a curse that triggers price collapse – certainly not cause for the peaceful and generous thoughts that food Modernists of the 1940s dreamed would come from an era of plenty. This is the human and system failure that comes from the shotgun marriage between abundance and cut-throat competition in 1995, the year the World Trade Organization imposed deregulated global competition on food, previously assumed to be a vital necessity of life and culture and thereby exempted from 'free trade' pressures.

Like everybody in the food sector, berry farmers are caught in the vortex of cheap food. Cheap food is the Tyrannosaurus Rex in the room that never gets discussed in polite company. It's not named during debates about free trade, the WTO or multi-billion-dollar subsidies to US and European farmers. A cheap food policy is never an election issue or subjected to a formal vote in legislatures. Cheap food just goes without saying – like it goes without saying that migrant workers without basic rights do the heavy lifting at fruit and vegetable farms, or that ships transport cheap food using the cheapest and most polluting fuels, or that WTO trade rules override UN human rights declarations, just a few items that authorities turn a blind eye to in a cheap food regime. As with Harry Potter's arch-villain, 'he who must not be named', cheap food has the power not to be known.

Cheap food

Though some date the origins of cheap food policy to the bread and circuses of the ancient Roman Empire, the modern prototype comes from the dawn of British industrialism, also a time of imperial conquest that brought cheap sugar, tea, coffee and later white bread within reach of early factory workers. They got four boosts from the new foods: a jolt of caffeine to send them off to work alert (quite a change from the effect of the traditional breakfast drink, ale); a quick hit of energy to fuel their bodies for the workshift; a fast meal of bread and jam munched on the way out the door, displacing the traditional but time-consuming family breakfast of cooked cereal; and perhaps the cheap thrill of belonging to an empire on top of the world.

Cheap food had a gigantic ripple effect. Cheap sugar came from enslaving Africans and transporting them to plantations in the Caribbean, where the original inhabitants were removed to make way for the conquerors. Cheap tea came from subjugating India. Cheap grains drove the opening of the North American frontier west, driving out the original inhabitants, largely to create space for immigrants driven off their land in Britain by competition with cheap grain from the Americas. By reducing a major cost item in the budget of working people, cheap food substituted for other social policies that could have sustained urban and factory life – minimum wages or social housing, for example, as was done in parts of continental Europe where a more complex 'welfare state' evolved. Instead of taxing the rich for social costs of industrialism or setting standards for wages in the leading 'workshop of the world', cheap food allowed these expenses to be outsourced to disadvantaged people in other countries who bore the burdens of delivering cheap product.[1]

Finding the control room of Britain's cheap food policy is impossible. Was it slavery that delivered cheap food? Was it the triumph of free trade during the 1840s and the subsequent 'informal empire' that roped farmers in the Americas into supplying cheap grains? Cheap food was a complex more than a policy. Perhaps the point to make is that no-one was ever so ill-considered as actually to conceive and plan a system with so many negative consequences. But cheap food did come out of a culture of mechanistic utilitarianism, as was rampant during industrialism.

Gluttons for punishment

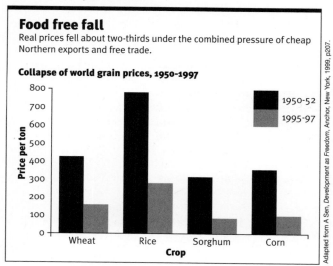

Food free fall

Real prices fell about two-thirds under the combined pressure of cheap Northern exports and free trade.

Collapse of world grain prices, 1950-1997

Price per ton — Crop

■ 1950-52
▨ 1995-97

Adapted from A Sen, Development as Freedom, Anchor, New York, 1999, p207.

The industrialized body needed 'fuel' for its motor. As in the world of English science and physics, food energy was measured in 'calories' that performed what physicists called 'work'.

Cheap food would not have played as well in a society where the body is understood as a temple, needing life energy, *prana* or *chi* from the universe. Nor does it fit in a biologically attuned culture – biology followed the rise of industrialism and economics in Britain – which appreciates the many complex nutrient needs of humans, beyond quick-burning fuel, or which values the body's ability to enjoy food sensually, with all six senses, or which appreciates mealtime as meeting the needs of a social animal for company – company, with its Latin roots for 'with' and 'bread'. Cheap food took hold in a public culture divorced from understanding that food was an essential of life – as essential to cultural heritage, rural survival, emergency planning, overall economic planning, ecological biodiversity and spiritual connectivity as it was to delivering work energy to the employer. A cheap food complex goes deep into a society, one reason why it's no easy, or purely logical, matter to change.

The empire strikes back

Major elements of the British cheap food complex remained in force in Britain and its settler colonies in Australia, New Zealand and North America throughout the 1800s and 1900s. But cheap food took on renewed importance during the early 1970s when it became pivotal to a major restructuring of the US and world economy. Pioneering analysis by Philip McMichael traces the change to the team around US President Richard Nixon foreseeing the need to reorient the US economy. The US could lead in exports of high-technology manufacturing, such as munitions, and in capital-intensive food exports, such as wheat and cotton. The rest was best done by others with cheaper and more disciplined workers, cheaper and less strict environmental regulations, and cheaper and less democratically checked politicians and employers.[2]

This was a fundamental rethink of the economic power base of economies. Traditional colonialism set up a dependency 'debt trap' which locked colonial hinterlands into exporting low-cost raw materials to the imperial center, which then exported more expensive manufactured goods to the colonies, indebting them again. By contrast, the post-1970s schema valued former colonies for their low wages, strong work ethic, docile unions and weak environmental standards – all disappearing from the West at the time, and all ideal for manufacturing. So, next-generation factories went South, leaving behind the low-wage service sector, which had no choice but to stay close to the customers it served.

In this scenario, farmers in the North took advantage

of large farms, advanced technology and public infrastructure to export cheap grains, dairy and meat to the
South. Workers in neocolonial factories of the South
got by on low wages by eating low-cost food grown
in the formerly industrialized North. Poorly paid consumers in the North got manufactured imports made
by underpaid Southern labor, thanks to a constant
influx of new Southern factory workers, driven off
their land by cheap imports of Northern food. Cheap
food rejigged social and economic structures as well as
trade patterns of both North and South.

By 1994, a year before the WTO came into effect,
a tiny percentage of US farms (2 per cent) accounted
for 64 per cent of world trade in corn, 40 per cent of
soy, 36 per cent of wheat, 33 per cent of cotton and
17 per cent of rice. By 2003, countries still commonly
referred to as industrial exported $321 billion worth
of foodstuffs, 74 per cent of their agricultural earnings;
by comparison, countries of the Global South, usually
depicted as pre-industrial, exported $138 billion worth
of foodstuffs, only 19 per cent of their agricultural
earnings.[3]

Stormy times
The changeover to a political economy based on a
global exchange of cheap food and cheap manufactured goods coincided with the stormy geopolitics of
the early 1970s, when resource shortages were con-
founded by cataclysmic rhetoric and confrontational
politics. World population, edging close to four billion in 1970, was often referred to as the 'population
bomb'. A new leadership from former 'developing'
or 'colonial' governments said the world was divided
between North and South, haves and have-nots, and
declared themselves a 'third world', no longer pawns
of the first and second worlds of Capitalists and
Communists. Arab countries jacked up oil prices in
1973 to retaliate against Western support for Israeli

expansion, and the ensuing 'oil shock' pushed up the price of most products. The world economy was stuck in 'stagflation', a double whammy of unemployment and inflation. The Modernist era of continuous progress seemed to hit a wall, which a classic report in 1972 called *The Limits to Growth*.

Food wasn't far from the storm center. The global harvest declined in 1972, followed by horrific famines in Ethiopia and Bangladesh and food shortages in about 20 countries. Emergency grain reserves dropped to 26 days supply. Wheat prices shot up sixfold, affecting the price of milk and meat, both dependent on low-cost grains. Oil price increases had the same impact on costs of fertilizer, pesticides and irrigation – the three pillars of Modernist high-input, high production agriculture during the 1950s and 1960s. To ensure food for the home population, the US and several European countries banned or limited food exports.

For power brokers such as Henry Kissinger, Nixon's Secretary of State, this turmoil was a crash course in international politics as an exercise in raw economic power. 'Control the oil and you control entire nations,' Kissinger would say, with an eye to the Arab monopoly over low-cost oil. 'Control the food and you control the people,' he'd continue, confident of US supremacy in that field. Food became the US checkmate to the strategic power of Arab oil. 'Hungry men listen only to those who have a piece of bread,' Nixon's agriculture secretary Earl Butz said. 'Food is a tool. It is a weapon in the US negotiating list.'

US President Gerald Ford (Nixon's replacement after he was forced to resign by the Watergate scandal) spoke to the UN General Assembly in September 1974 on 'allocation of the world's resources'. Ford warned the countries of the South against overplaying the energy card, lest countries of the North withheld food. Ford laid out four principles for a price stabilizing deal: double the output of food and energy; keep energy and food prices low; renounce use of any commodities as political weapons; share low-cost food from the developed world with the world's poor. This policy of cheap and freely traded energy and food has guided the US orientation toward world resources ever since.

Kissinger orchestrated a World Food Conference in Rome that November, with hopes of developing a consensus on long-term policy trade-offs. In his keynote address, he expressed Ford's themes in idealistic rhetoric, pledging that 'within a decade, no man, woman or child will go to bed hungry.' Talk could be even cheaper than food.[4]

Cannon-fodder food

The US-inspired 1970s' sequel to British-style cheap food was a reinvention, not a rehash. The original centered on low-cost grains, sugar and tea. The 1970s' version included significant amounts of meat, dairy, sugar and oils. That change reflected a major shift in dietary thinking since the 1890s. When English youth raised on sweet nothings tried to sign up for military service in the period from the 1890s to 1914, they were unfit for battle, creating panic that the safety of the Empire was endangered if nutrition did not improve. Serving as military cannon-fodder was more demanding on bodies than factory work, and this raised patriotic awareness of the need for strong bones, red-blooded virility and muscular strength, which required iron, calcium and protein from dairy and meat. (With cannon-fodder, there was little need to worry about diet-based chronic diseases when people aged.)

Military standards of dietary adequacy for civilian and troop morale became commonplace throughout the West by the 1940s. Food guides were adopted in many countries during World War Two. The US school meals act of 1946 was explicitly motivated as a way to ensure the health of future recruits. Changes to food production technology meant there was no need to turn the clock back on meat and dairy in order to provide cheap food during the 1970s. The cost of meat and dairy stayed low thanks to cheap grains that fattened livestock quickly, reducing the time to watch over grazing herds and the turnover time to fatten animals up. Even though the proportion of US income spent on food went down substantially from 1900 to the late 1970s, meat and dairy consumption stayed steady, grain declined, while sugar and fat from vegetable oils went up.[5]

Another area of reinvention related to women's rights. The early British version predated women having the right to vote or to work at many jobs outside the home. But the sequel adapted to new realities. Cheap processed foods were depicted as a convenience revolution that liberated women from the drudgery of unpaid housework. With processed foods to help, women no longer had to stay at home just to cook dinner. This shift fit perfectly with the shift across the North to a labor-intensive service and office workforce after the 1970s, a de-industrialized workforce in which a male no longer earned a 'living wage' to support his family. Once families needed two full-time incomes to manage, something had to give, and that was food preparation – prior to the 1970s, a relentless set of time-consuming chores that kept one spouse fully occupied at home. Food that stayed cheap – even when it was picked up on the run, ready to heat and eat, even when it was served in a restaurant with a clown and a playground for the kids, even if everyone in the house ate separately because there was no common time for family meals – came to the rescue of both two-income and one-parent families, in which adults worked more hours than they did before the cheap food revolution that liberated them. The 'value added' was convenience, a word that put a positive spin on the time famine that obsesses two-income families. Processed, prepared and take-out meals became the ultimate in supporting cheap labor, because they allowed two paid workers to earn enough to support a family that one paid and one unpaid parent had supported before.

Food processing

Food itself was reinvented by the 1970s' cheap food revolution. The reduced cost of meals that came with more processing and service was made possible in part by reductions in the amount of the food dollar that went to farmers for actual food. US farmers, for example, got 37 cents on the food dollar in 1973, but less than 20 cents after 2000. The ability of processors to deliver prefab food without raising prices raises the question: is cheap food cheap despite being processed, or because it is processed? Readers of Michael Pollan's exposé of the 'corn-ucopian' dystopia behind cheap food will appreciate that processed food is cheap precisely because it uses the multiple personalities of corn to stand in for functions and tastes otherwise performed by more expensive real foods. The more processing, the more corn, the less money spent on actual food, the cheaper the meal – that's the economic recipe.

That's why grains and meat, not fruit and vegetables, remain the foundation of a cheap food diet. Grains can be converted to cheap meat by feeding them to livestock penned up in factory barns. And grains can be stretched so that four cents of corn provide four dollars of cornflakes, 27 cents of potatoes cost $3.40 in potato chips and 2.6 cents of corn provides four dollars' worth of corn chips. Fruits and vegetables, which should be the foundation of a healthy diet, are not the foundations of a 'value-added' processed food industry. By 2002, world sales of processed foods came to $3.2 trillion.[6]

There's another major difference between the old and the new in cheap food. The original happened when food retailers and processors were small-scale and regional, and when canning, then less than 50 years old, was about as far as food manufacturing went. By the 1970s, a handful of global oligopolies could produce, transform and retail a wide range of foods across continents. By 2004, 15 corporations controlled almost a fifth of all packaged foods. Backstage, the same pattern of corporate concentration typifies all players in the food chain – except for food producers and consumers, who are on their own when they face these conglomerates at opposite ends of the food system. Ten seed companies control seeds, for example, while five trading companies control grain sales, ten pesticide companies control pesticides, and so on.

Despite the clout of these seemingly powerful input manufacturers and processors, the shift to cheap food coincided with an inter-corporate power shift from input suppliers and processors to retailers. After the 1970s, supermarkets established the pecking order. Since they controlled access to customers, they told processors what price points to meet for what quantities, and the processors passed the burden down the line to farmers. Monopolies with bulk purchasing power became the enforcers of cheap food.

Despite high levels of corporate concentration, the cheap food system rules the roost, not the giant corporations. In the days of managerial capitalism that JK Galbraith famously analyzed during the 1950s and 1960s, monopolies used their power to demand higher prices, a portion of which were shared with workers. Few food monopolies are that lucky these days. Since the era of cheap food, the norm has been cut-throat competition among monopolies vying for market share by discounting. Cheap food controls monopolies, not the other way around. Indeed, cheap food creates monopolies because the only way companies can survive low margins is with huge volumes. Monopolies become bigger because volume is about the only survival factor they can influence.[7]

Gluttons for punishment

McModernism

I call this 1970s' phase of cheap food McModernist, to distinguish it from the more heroic Modernist phase of chapter 1. Like Modernism, it uses technology to create surplus and lower prices, and to release people from tradition and natural limits. But it also departed from 1950s' Modernism, which was based on a virtuous circle of mutual prosperity. McModernism works on a virtuous circle from Hell – technology and infrastructure allow Northern farmers to sell cheap grains, meats and dairy products into Southern markets; low-cost imported food keeps poorly paid Southern factory workers alive; a continuous flow of fresh recruits from the countryside to work in Southern factories keeps Southern wages low after workers lost their farms to competition from cheap food imports; cheap manufactured goods from the South sell to low-waged Northern workers. Economic analyst Greg Albo calls it 'competitive austerity,' which draws companies and countries into 'beggar-thy-neighbor' methods that eventually lead to mutually assured destruction, between companies and countries. 'Competition in the new global economy' has become a stock phrase that covers up the reality that we have more food than we know what to do with because the only thing we know how to do is compete.[8]

As with English cheap food during the 1800s, US and later European cheap food since the 1970s have been part of a complex. The complex has not prevailed as a result of sheer efficiency being expressed through markets. Cheap food depended on government-funded foreign aid to whet the whistle of people in Southern countries for Northern grains and dairy. It relied on public subsidies for university research, energy and transportation. It took export subsidies for grains, which are exported as stand-alone products and as feedstock for livestock. Cheap food depended on aggressive campaigns by Northern governments to lower

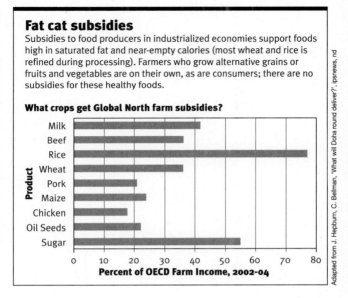

Fat cat subsidies

Subsidies to food producers in industrialized economies support foods high in saturated fat and near-empty calories (most wheat and rice is refined during processing). Farmers who grow alternative grains or fruits and vegetables are on their own, as are consumers; there are no subsidies for these healthy foods.

What crops get Global North farm subsidies?

(bar chart, Product vs. Percent of OECD Farm Income, 2002-04)

- Milk
- Beef
- Rice
- Wheat
- Pork
- Maize
- Chicken
- Oil Seeds
- Sugar

Percent of OECD Farm Income, 2002-04

protective barriers against imports in the Global South. It relied on government tolerance of global monopolies with power to determine patterns of international trade, because most international trade is simply a transfer of goods on the supply chain of one corporation. Finally, cheap food relied on a food culture divorced from tradition and parenting, featuring stock ingredients such as sugar, a few grains, dairy and meat, many prepared for heating and eating. Thanks to the interplay of such factors, the US and Europe competed in 2003 for top spot in exports of cereals, meat and milk; the US led the world with oilseeds, citrus and fibers, while Europe took a big lead on sugar – the opposite of what might be expected from industrialized countries.[9]

'Lifestyle' eating

Unfortunately, cheap food came on the scene in the very decade that public health advocates shifted to a more conciliatory advocacy strategy. From the 1880s to 1960s, public health was known for promoting legislative change – improved handling of sewage, garbage, food adulteration, conditions leading to contagious disease, and so on, initiating the first breakthroughs in what came to be known as the welfare state. But during the 1970s, as so-called 'diseases of affluence' became more evident – many cases of heart disease and cancer were considered diseases of excess rather than deficiency – public health leaders turned their attention to 'lifestyle' decisions that individuals needed to make. In the nutrition field, this shift was associated with dropping of hard-lined approaches to regulating corporations. All foods fit, it was said, and 'breast is best', implying that formula might be second best, which isn't so very bad. A little step from there, and the acceptable dietary advice became something like 'choose more lean meats', rather than 'reduce meat consumption'. The food industry fought anything that smacked of 'less'. As long as 'choose more' got in, the sales pitch for cheap food had a chance, it was thought. Public health has yet to recover from those decades of accommodation to cheap food and the decline of advocacy based on awareness of the public policy and economic determinants of health and well-being. As a result, cheap food came on the scene facing very little resistance.[10]

Long before the Soviet Union collapsed, cheap food during the 1970s established a new world odor and order by flipping which countries did what kind of production. According to Philip McMichael's path-breaking analysis, the reorganization of the world economy ended the post-World War Two 'development project' of creating rounded, diverse and balanced high-tech economies throughout the world. Instead, the planet was split between an ostensibly 'under-developed' world that exported cheap manufactured goods and a few food specialties to a 'developed' world that exported cheap food and munitions back – a pretty significant change of a planetary agenda to happen without transparency or public input.

'Teach a man to trade'

Like the invisible hand of a market that went unrecognized until Adam Smith named its power, cheap food awaits its Adam Smith. Hidden from view by an invisibility cloak, cheap food has avoided recognition as the defining systemic force behind the bellwether controversies about global food, trade, health, equity and environment trends since the 1980s. For instance, the Tyrannosaurus Rex of a cheap food complex did not get discussed in *Our Common Future*, a landmark publication of the World Commission on Environment and Development in 1987, best known for the phrase 'sustainable development'.

The least developed and poorest countries still specialize in raw material and food exports, the *Common Future* report noted. From three to six transnational corporations control prices of basic commodities, which fell by half between 1980 and 1985, causing poor countries 'to subsidize the wealthier importers', the report said. The environmental consequence of playing musical chairs with manufacturing and transferring it to the Global South amounted to an export of pollution, the report said. It would have added $14.2 billion to the yearly bill for manufactured exports if Southern pollution-control equipment met minimal Northern standards. The report also criticized US and European subsidies that led to dumping their food surpluses on the South. But *Our Common Future* did not weave its individual points into a pattern. This low level of pattern recognition was a missed opportunity to educate the public about the systemic unsustainability of a two-way trade scheme, the driving purpose of which is to swap cheap food for cheap manufactured goods.[11]

Gluttons for punishment

Nor has awareness of this cheap food trading pattern been raised in many public policy debates since. It certainly can't compete with the popularity of a famous one-liner dropped by some unknown person on the best way to help poor people in the developing world. Give a man a fish and you feed him for a day, the line went, but teach him to fish, and you feed him forever. The advice sounds so patronizing today that it's funny. People play with it, with lines such as 'teach a man to fish and you get rid of him every weekend.' But the original advice was a metaphor – I doubt anyone believed that poor people didn't know how to fish – that came out of the development era of the 1950s, when it was thought all countries would develop, become mature, self-reliant and equal through productive work and trade. No-one would give such advice in today's world. Why give any fish to poor people when you can give them corndogs, and sell the lean and healthy fish protein to rich people? Teach a man to fish, and he can feed Northerners forever, is today's advice.

Bono and Bob

Those hooked on the fish story like the idea that 'trade, not aid' will help countries climb out of poverty. Aside from the usual suspects, such as the World Bank and the World Trade Organization, those promoting barrier-free trade include famous rockers such as Bono and Bob Geldof, associated with the compelling Make Poverty History campaign of 2005. The media gave full play to Bono and Geldof's campaign to pressure a meeting in Scotland of leaders of the world's eight wealthiest countries. Geldof said three policies could make poverty history and fix Africa's problems 'in ten seconds' – cancel paralyzing debts to international bankers, raise foreign aid, and end the subsidies and barriers that block African exporters from financing development through trade, not aid.

I was at a conference in Dublin on peak oil and food security at the time, and asked quite a few people for their thoughts on Bono and Geldof. If increased trade solved anything, replied Darrin Qualman, research director of Canada's National Farmers' Union, Canadian farmers would be the poster children. They increased foreign grain sales from $10.9 billion in 1988 to $28.2 billion in 2002. But farm income dropped by 24 per cent, and farm debt for fertilizer and other inputs doubled. Farmers always get the wrong end of the stick in an export economy, said Qualman, because they compete for sales with goods grown by a billion farmers, while everything they buy comes from three or four monopolies. 'The farm income crunch is caused by this imbalance of market power in the global food chain,' he says, which will work the same way on Africa's chocolate, cotton and coffee producers. The issue for Africa, Qualman said, was 'the right to build barriers, not tear them down'.

Annie Sugrue, who headed the South African community economic development group, Eco City, scoffed at the idea that trade would benefit a population where 46 per cent of the people survive on less than a dollar a day. 'It's complete rubbish to say they're going to be involved in trade,' she says. All of South Africa's clothing workers lost their jobs to imports from China, she adds. 'If anyone wants to help Africa, they should cancel trade, not just the debt.' European trade barriers to African food exports actually help the poor in Africa, she says, because they force local farmers to grow food for the local market instead of flowers for Europe.

No way trade

A careful read of UN Food and Agriculture Organization (FAO) research, as distinct from policy, confirms Qualman's and Sugrue's scorn for trade-based food strategies. FAO's 2004 report documents that Southerners are exploited by powerful

Gluttons for punishment

multinational monopolies: if export prices had stayed stable since 1980, Southern countries would have earned an additional $112 billion in 2002, more than double the amount received in foreign aid. What happened to the $112 billion? 'At the international level, a few vertically integrated companies have gained increasing control over agricultural trade,' and get the lion's share of money spent by Northern consumers, the report noted. 'Even with bananas, which require almost no processing, international trading companies, distributors and retailers claim 88 per cent of the retail price,' while 'barely two per cent' goes to plantation workers, the FAO reported. Yet, one year later, an FAO study promoted trade as the way out of poverty. The FAO campaigns regularly for free trade, cuts in subsidies for Northern farmers, and phasing out regulations that make it hard for processed foods from the South to enter Northern markets.[12]

China's food assembly

If food exports and free trade offered a way out of poverty, China should be a shining example. It has the population base for mass production. It has diplomatic clout. It has a literate and disciplined workforce. It has a highly respected tradition of excellence in agriculture and food. China's shrewd food exporters know where they fit in the Western food system, which assembles inputs, as often as not chemicals, more than foods. After four decades of cheap food and better living through biochemistry, Westerners don't buy food any more. They buy processed meals assembled from ingredients or inputs.

The strategy, therefore, is to bundle, rather than grow or make, the result of an around-the-world-in-80-ingredients mishmash that economists refer to as 'vertical disintegration of production across borders', the key to modern global foods as much as to global cars. With an eye to input power, China moved to control as many inputs as possible, and became the dominant player in such items as vitamins B and C, garlic, apples, apple juice, farmed fish, processed fish, honey, onions and organic broccoli. The world food, just like the world car, is assembled close to a major point of sale so people can buy the product their neighbors made. So China-sourced honey, dried berries and vitamins B and C can be added to Canadian wheat flakes in a prepared cereal, and packaged as a product of Canada, since the biggest cost is Canadian assembly and packaging.[13]

China offers low wages and low environmental standards the Global North can't match. When products require precision hand labor at low wages, Chinese exporters do it. They do salmon, which have 36 pin bones best handled by hand, and crab, best removed by hand with pincers. No-one costs the pollution from shipping and refrigerating salmon and crab from the North American west coast to China and then back. And few stop to ask who gets hurt most in this world of wage-based competition that is supposed to lead the way out of poverty.

Here's how one downward spiral unravels. China's cheap apples and apple juice beat out once-prized apples from western North America in North American markets; unsold apples from western North America are then dumped in India, bankrupting Indian apple producers. The world's farmers are turned into competitors with each other, transporting goods, mostly composed of water, back and forth around the world – transactions that are high in energy use but low in added value to health or social well-being. As for the impact of this export strategy in China, a 2006 report from China's National Development and Reform Commission documented stark inequalities. China's inequality between city and country 'would make many a modern capitalist blush', *The Economist* comments in an article on the report. The share of Gross

Gluttons for punishment

Domestic Product going to wages declined from 53 to 41 per cent during the period when exports exploded, from 1998 to 2005. Even when food exports are pursued by a powerful state following a shrewd strategy, China's experience shows, the relentless downward pressures of the global cheap food system prevail.[14]

Korean routes

South Korea provides a different kind of case study. Korea is one of the 'Asian Tigers' – Hong Kong, Taiwan and Singapore are others – a small group that broke free of colonialism to become hubs of sophisticated industries and therefore a success story worthy of study. The tiny peninsula is a star performer in many areas, including its healthy diet, featuring spicy *kimchi*, considered one of the world's superfoods. Though classified as undeveloped as recently as the 1950s, it is now one of the top ten industrial powers in the world. Analysts of Korea's achievements give credit to an active state that planned industrial clusters strategically and invested heavily in education and social equality, factors usually left to look after themselves in typical promotions of export-led growth.

Despite urban and industrial successes, Korea's three-and-a-half million farmers are deeply troubled. Their pain was brought to world attention in 2003 when Lee Kyang Hae, a leading spokesperson for Korean farmers, chose the day of Korea's harvest celebration to stab himself to death outside a meeting of the World Trade Organization in Cancún, Mexico. About a hundred of his Korean friends sat down by his side and raised a banner in his honor, 'WTO Kills', a reference to the desperate situation of farmers forced to compete in their own home market against highly subsidized exports from the US and Europe.[15]

I was invited to South Korea to speak on local routes to food security in October 2006, just after North

Korea tested its new nuclear weaponry. Environmental groups in South Korea were equally worried that food security and rural sustainability would blow up if a proposed bilateral free trade deal with the US was adopted, providing full frontal exposure to US cheap food. After the conference, Denise, a local organizer, takes me to meet members of a farm organization in a tiny mountain village called Deok-bong-san, about an hour by train from Seoul. We stroll up the hill to the village restaurant and meet She-ik Oh, introduced to me by Denise as a member of the local farmers' organization. He bows to me, and flashes a grin at Denise. 'I am a peasant, not a farmer,' he says to her in Korean. 'Farmers work for money. Peasants work because they love the land and are tied to it.' Who could ask for a better introduction?

We leave our shoes at the restaurant door and I meet several executive members of the local peasants' and farmers' league. Our room has a long table on short legs. Dread overtakes me. My inner Westerner, raised in a chair-based culture of the dinner table, flinches at sitting cross-legged on the floor, and I prepare to accept gracious Asian hospitality while hiding the pain from my bad back and tight hips. I meet my new friends without shoes or chairs to keep us apart or separate us from free-flowing relations with the energy of our space. We share food laid out for everyone to share, instead of each person getting an individual serving on their own plate. Though my flesh is weak, my spirit appreciates how the very architecture of Korean meals allows us to rub shoulders in a free-flowing food culture.

After a few minutes of chatting, the president of the local league asks how old I am. That's a weird question to ask so soon, I say to myself before giving the answer. A bottle of 'farmers' wine' – a milk-like potion that farmers enjoy at lunch, claiming it gives them extra energy – is set on the table. Everyone pours a drink for someone else, never for themselves. A nice touch of togetherness, I think. Then I notice that the person pouring my drink uses two hands instead of one, a mark of respect for the oldest person at the table. Respect for culture, tradition and community infuse Korean meals.

No obesity

Far from being obsolete, Korean dishes may become the model for eco-superfoods of the coming century. Almost every serving embodies high-nutrient, low-calorie goodness, which may explain why I never saw one obese person during a nine-day tour of Korea's cities and countryside. Most dishes also express a food system that is as close to nature as it is to culture. At the center of the table, which everyone can reach with chopsticks, there's a bowl of pork, commonly raised on food scraps rather than grains, and several dishes of fish, shellfish and seaweed from the ocean, an hour's drive away. About ten veggie dishes are passed around – tofu, sweet potato, cucumber (grown by my peasant friend, She-ik), mushrooms, several varieties of kimchi (cabbage fermented with ginger, red chili pepper and garlic), lettuce, collards, and carrots. A range of green leaves are used as low-calorie wraps in place of bread. Many dishes use parts of a plant that would be wasted in North America – leaves of squash used as wraps, or persimmon leaves used in tea, for example. Several dishes, such as miso and kimchi, are fermented, a low-tech and low-energy form of preservation that adds healthy enzymes to food.

Korea's special national foods are eaten daily, not just on rare holidays. These identity foods evolved from a frugal folk culture based on local ingredients cooked at home from scratch. Though Korea is ultra-modern in its technology, education, clothing, entertainments and politics, food still expresses tradition that predates mechanization, long-haul transportation, processing, packaging, microwaving of prepared foods and eating alone.

Rice rules

Meat is not the center of the meal. Rice is. We each have our own silver bowl, and Denise discreetly elbows me to make sure I finish mine and sing its praises. Rice is a specialty of the area, in a country where rice is a sacramental staple – used in rice wine, rice cakes and an after-dinner drink of sweet rice water left after the cooking, as well as eaten in its own bowl at every meal. Western Christians who give thanks for their daily bread have an inkling of understanding, but not a three-times-a-day ritual, of how a staple can fill people with identity, spirituality and culture.

After lunch, we stroll up to the home of the wealthiest farmer in the village, who raises over 20 cows (they don't raise steers as in North America and Europe, since cows provide both meat and offspring) for meat. We sip pineleaf tea fermented in honey, with a few pine nuts tossed in. The pines and the mountain ranges they cover are symbols of permanence, disturbed only by a few Buddhist temples, rarely by monster homes. Like many iconic Korean foods – ginseng and green tea are best known – pine tea and honey are foraged from the mountains that occupy two-thirds of the landscape. Korean food has the taste of Korea's sea, land and mountains.

A brief tour of farms along the valley reveals many farms of only a few hectares, most of which make full use of space by growing vegetables in low-tech greenhouses. Rice farms are mostly about ten hectares. I watch the rice being harvested by a small crew with a combine, leased by day from the Government, a shrewd way to keep capital costs down in a small operation. To save farm space, the rice is dried on canvas by the side of the country road. Despite rich soil, hard work, deep knowledge and careful use of resources, everyone I speak with expresses sadness that their children never think of taking up a low-wage future in farming. Everyone blames their plight on cheap imports from the US, one of the world's leading rice exporters, and shudders with fear as to their future if a free trade deal with the US is passed.

Protests from threatened Korean peasants and US industries delayed negotiation of a trade deal in time for fast-track approval by President George W Bush. But such trade deals are likely in Asia's future. Anyone who's tracked the tobacco industry knows how it shifted its sights to Asia as soon as health alarms went off in Europe and North America during the 1960s. The same survival strategy for obsolete industries applies to junk food, which also needs fresh and unprepared markets to conquer. Free trade deals allow in cheap carbs and meat from afar, and that wedge scrapes off the top layers of fragile folk systems of eating, engaging with food and living. When the top layer has been scraped, other products that require deeper incisions will follow in convenience stores and supermarkets that are already there.

This is why food sovereignty, a capacity to act as a collective to defend food security, is moving to center-stage in the global resistance to cheap food. And it's why new business models, new ecological and self-reliance ethics, and new lifestyle strategies and purchasing habits are spreading – the theme of the coming chapter.

1 S Mintz, *Sweetness and Power* (Penguin, 1986). **2** P McMichael, *Development and Social Change: A Global Perspective* (Pine Forge Press, 2000). **3** P McMichael, 'Global Food Politics', in *Monthly Review*, Vol 50 No 3 July-August 1998; FAO, *The State of Food and Agriculture*, 2005, p 172. **4** S Brown, *The Faces of Power: Constancy and Change in United States Foreign Policy* (Columbia University Press, 1994) p 290; *Time* magazine, 25 Nov 1974; *Time*, 11 Nov 1974; G Ford, 'Allocation of the World's Resources', in *Encyclopedia Britannica Profiles: The American Presidency*, 1974. **5** G Cannon, 'The Fate of Nations: Food and nutrition policy in the new world,' *Caroline Walker Lecture*, 2003; USDA, 'Nutrient Content of the US Food Supply, 2005', in *Home Economics Research Report*, No 58, March 2008, pp 12-16. **6** T Winson, *The Intimate Commodity* (Garamond Press, 1995); M Vander Stichele and S van der Wal, *The Profit Behind Your Plate: Critical Issues in the Processed Food Industry* (SOMO, 2006) p13, 15, 33; Debbie Barker, *The Rise and Predictable Fall of Globalized Industrial Agriculture* (International Forum on Globalization, 2007), p7; H Schaffer et al, 'US Agricultural Commodity Policy and its Relationship to Obesity', Background Paper developed for the Wingspread Conference, March 2007. **7** J Kolko, *Restructuring the World Economy* (Pantheon, 1988). **8** G Albo, 'Competitive Austerity and the Impasse of Capitalist Employment Policy', in R Miliband and L Panitch, *Socialist Register* 30 (Merlin Press,1994); G Albo, 'A World Market of Opportunities? Capitalist Obstacles and Left Economic Policy,' in L Panitch, ed, *Socialist Register* 33 (Merlin Press, 1997). **9** FAO, *The State of Agricultural Commodity Markets*, 2004, pp 41-3. **10** See M Pollan, *In Defense of Food: An Eater's Manifesto* (Penguin, 2008); M Nestle, *Food Politics* (University of California Press, 2002); G Cannon, 'The Fate of Nations: Food and Nutrition Policy in the New World', *Caroline Walker Lecture*, 2003. **11** World Commission on Environment and Development, *Our Common Future* (Oxford University Press, 1988), pp 80-88, 118-24. **12** FAO, *The State of Agricultural Commodity Markets 2004*, especially pp 14, 31; FAO, *The State of Food and Agriculture 2005* (SOFA, 2005); OECD, *Agricultural Trade and Poverty* (OECD, 2003). **13** 'Economics Focus, An old Chinese myth', in *The Economist* 5 January 2008, p 75; 'How Fit is the Panda?,' *The Economist*, 29 September 2007; 'The great unbundling', *The Economist*, 20 January 2007. For daily coverage of Chinese food safety practices, go to www.foodsafetynetwork.ca archives, and search 'China.' **14** G York, 'China frets over widening income disparity' in *Globe and Mail*, 9 February 2006, p 1, 18; *The Economist*, 13 October 2007, p 15, 90. **15** D Rodrik, 'Getting Interventions Right: How South Korea and Taiwan Grew Rich', in *National Bureau of Economic Research*, Working Paper 4964, 1994; R Wade, *Growing the Market: Economic Theory and the Role of Government in East Asian Industrialization* (Princeton University Press, 2003).

6 Economics as if food mattered

Cheap food comes at a high cost to health, the environment and community economic development. When we understand this market failure, we can see why alternatives to cheap food can offer higher value and a better deal for a relatively small additional cost.

YOU DON'T REALLY understand something, Stuart Hill used to say, until you know its paradox. An early alternative thinker among Canadian professors at agriculture schools, Hill would have fun thinking about the paradoxes bedeviling cheap food.

Paradoxically, cheap food is very expensive. The sticker price at the store may be low. The percentage of income going to food may be low. The full, or life-cycle, cost of cheap food, however, 'from grow it to throw it', is another matter. Cheap food is an elaborate 'buy now, pay later' sales scheme. After paying a bargain price at the cash register come at least several charges no-one bargained for. Once individuals and groups understand the real expense of cheap food, they are open to paying more of the full cost upfront. The thoughts and actions behind food producers and consumers doing just that, without much help from governments or large corporations, are the subject of this chapter.

The paradox of expensive cheap food comes from hidden costs that most people don't see or anticipate. There are five kinds of these hidden costs, which are worth reviewing to get a sense of the size of the pot of money that is now wasted on hidden costs but could be used in a more creative way – to stimulate the conditions that make food a many-splendored thing. The new economics of global food is about making that switch.

Hidden costs

The first hidden costs flow from the principle that 'what goes around comes around'. Cheap food gets people coming and going. There's a low-priced aisle for foods that have had fiber removed, and a high-priced aisle for laxatives, antacids and upset tummy remedies. Junk costs as much to get rid of as to buy. British taxpayers pay $85 million a year to cover laxatives for seniors, a fraction of the cost paid by all suffering from constipation. These expenses can be avoided by eating real food that comes with its own roto-rooter, the fiber that processors take out. Perhaps de-fibered foods should carry warnings like the ones on toys that say the cost of batteries is separate: cost of enemas not included. Constipation reveals a food system that's stuck because it's only cheap and easy at the front end. Colon cancer, one out of a third of all cancers linked to poor diet, reveals the longer-term consequences. Since the additional expense is charged to a health rather than agricultural expenditure, the hidden subsidy to cheap food isn't visible.[1]

A second type of hidden expense comes due when governments pay for farm bail-outs. As with health spending, the government has its spending cycle backwards. Instead of positive farm incentives to get it right the first time, taxes pay for the financial crisis after the cheap food has left the barn. Because the money to subsidize cheap food is laundered through farmer bail-outs, it seems to be about helping farmers, not bailing out a dysfunctional cheap food system.

The third hidden cost of cheap food comes from the inevitable and expensive poverty, inequality and disruption that come from underpaying food workers. Since government programs to cope with the consequences of poverty are classified as social development or welfare, few people connect the dots to the ass-backwards design of a cheap food system. The rise of cheap food since the 1970s coincides with rising inequality throughout the world, including in relatively affluent countries where McJobs have displaced jobs that once paid a living wage. In the Global South, cheap food leads to two troubling migration trends of the last decades. First is the exodus of poor people from rural areas, what *Planet of Slums* author Mike Davis calls the 'mass production of slums' – a trend enveloping about 40 per cent of the people of the Global South. The irrational trend, an expression of desperation, depopulates one area to overpopulate another, forcing people to leave an area where costs of living are relatively low to seek work in an area where costs of land, housing and food are high.

The second migration trend turns the young and restless poor into nomads without a country. Until recently, most short-term migration for temporary farm jobs was to the Global North, where citizens turned up their noses at such hard work for such low wages. It's now estimated that over 70 million 'South to South' migrants are in transit, looking for

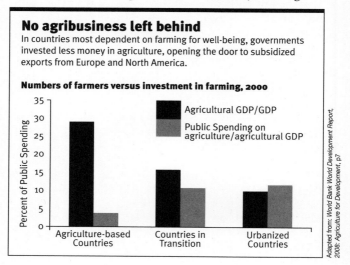

No agribusiness left behind

In countries most dependent on farming for well-being, governments invested less money in agriculture, opening the door to subsidized exports from Europe and North America.

Numbers of farmers versus investment in farming, 2000

Agricultural GDP/GDP

Public Spending on agriculture/agricultural GDP

(y-axis: Percent of Public Spending — 0, 5, 10, 15, 20, 25, 30, 35)

(x-axis categories: Agriculture-based Countries, Countries in Transition, Urbanized Countries)

Adapted from: World Bank World Development Report, 2008: Agriculture for Development, p7 seasonal farm work in another low-waged country of the Global South. Since the 1990s in Nicaragua, for example, some 500,000 people a year have been traveling throughout Central America to find seasonal farm jobs, a process that disrupts their personal, family and village life. Nicaraguan economist Francisco Mayorga describes the trend as a new form of pillaging the colonial world. The trend, argues respected Cornell University sociologist Philip McMichael, is no longer 'simply about producing cheap food'. Since cheap food imposes disorganization on the entire structure of economies and societies, 'it is also about securing new conditions for accumulation by lowering the cost of labor worldwide,' he argues.[2]

Environment suffers

The fourth hidden cost of cheap food comes from repairing damage to the environment after producers 'externalize' the costs of proper stewardship thanks to what's called a 'regulatory subsidy'. When producers 'externalize' a cost, they get rid of a problem they cause – by dumping manure in a river, rather than composting it, for example. When governments allow farmers and companies to cut their costs in this way, it's a regulatory subsidy. It's the cheapest and sleaziest way for a government to subsidize an industry, since no formal grants are required, just turning blind eyes.

Agriculture dumps eroded soil, manure and toxic residues into land, water and air. But some significant portion of the erosion, manure and toxins needs to be cleaned up before people drink the water and breathe the air, so taxpayers end up paying the cleaning bill after the regulatory subsidy. British farm analyst Jules Pretty worked up some estimates for a few clean-up costs and concluded that British taxpayers spend $45-$50 to clean up water damage passed on by every hectare of farmland. Giving that money to farmers to care properly for each hectare of land is what the campaign to turn regulatory subsidies into fees for environmental services is about.[3]

The fifth hidden cost of cheap food is harder to calculate financially. Many of the methods used to keep sticker prices down insult taste buds as well as health, as when jams are filled with more sugar than fruit, or 'plump' tomatoes are pumped up with water, or yeasty breads become vehicles to supplement flour with free air. The universal presence of salt, corn and seaweed – usually labeled according to the chemical property they provide rather than the product most people can recognize – testifies to the extent of product substitution in low-cost foods. If the label requires an advanced science degree to understand, the likelihood is that chemicals are standing in for real ingredients with more complex tastes.

The tragedy of the market

Cheap food has prevailed for some time because of 'market failures' compounded by political failures. Market failure refers to a 'collective action problem' that keeps sellers and buyers from co-operating to solve common problems that need to be solved. When everyone has to stand up at an outdoor concert because a few people at the front won't sit down, that's a lose-lose situation that comes from collective action problems in crowds. The hidden costs of cheap food indicate lose-lose situations that collective action needs to correct because market forces haven't been able to do so as pioneering work by Cecilia Rocha shows.[4]

Until recently, moving to correct market failures in the food and agriculture sector wasn't rocket science. Governments have long regulated food safety because companies couldn't get it together to police themselves to do it at a level the public trusted. Likewise, there are longstanding government programs to encourage farm research and education because private interests couldn't get their act together to sponsor these necessary programs. There used to be parallel programs to prevent free falls of food prices that threatened future food security and environmental quality. The original Modernists favored many of them. From 1947 to 1993, the General Agreement on Tariffs and Trade (GATT) permitted governments to assist and protect domestic farmers to protect their market share and ensure that they could produce food into the future. The rush to deregulate food policy after the World Trade Organization displaced GATT in 1995 trumped centuries of experience with food as a foundation stone of health, culture, community and the economy, relationships that couldn't be entirely trusted to or managed by market interests.[5]

Experience before and since 1995 confirms that market forces need public help to correct the cheap food spiral. The very nature of food and farming, not just the greed of individuals or corporations, pre-determines that self-regulation can't solve this problem.

How the market (doesn't) work

To start with, food goes bad or stale, sometimes quickly. No-one wants stale or sour food. So farmers start losing bargaining power every hour after the food is ready, especially at harvest time when all the farmers in an area have food they want to move fast. Few industries deal with such relentless pressures to sell fast at any price.

Second, farmers with expensive land or equipment to pay for face pressures to take any price that pays off the loans so their farm doesn't get seized. So when prices go down, farmers with big expensive tractors produce more, which makes prices fall even lower. Far from an investment in future rewards or food security for the population, spending on farm equipment turns farmers into price takers, not price makers.

Third, controlling supply is as hard as controlling climate, not as easy as shutting down an assembly line.

Economics

Perennial crops such as apples and grapes keep on coming, no matter what the price. Nor do cows stop giving milk, or hens stop laying eggs in response to market signals. Farmers are also perennials. When one farmer goes broke, a neighbor buys the land, so the amount of land never declines, just the number of farmers.

Even seemingly all-powerful corporations face these relentless pressures. Food shoppers don't look, then come back a week later and buy. In the food business, a missed sale is lost forever. That apple will be bought somewhere else. So that apple must be shined up and priced to sell, especially if it loses quality after a few more days on the shelf. Despite high levels of ownership concentration in the food industry, price wars are more common than co-operation or collusion to limit the cutthroat discounting that's cannibalizing many sectors of the food industry.

Farms go broke

University of Tennessee farm economist Daryll Ray has exposed the nooks and crannies of market failure in the food sector for over a decade. A 30-year wave of farm bankruptcies in the US, the global price leader in the food industry, 'is the direct result of expanding productive capacity while ignoring the need for policies to manage the use of that capacity,' Ray argues. Unwilling to manage supply – that would be intervening in the marketplace – the US Government dishes out subsidies to cover farm losses, which is apparently not intervening in the marketplace. Many governments in affluent countries follow suit, which accounts for $280 billion a year in farm subsidies spent in major industrial countries. Instead of blaming subsidies for falling prices, as do many free traders and a few charities, Ray blames government failure to manage falling prices for the subsidies.

Governments that are active with subsidies but inactive with supply management are, in Ray's view, selling the food store to grain traders, processors and meat packers who get to play with the wide margin between cheap grain costs and high costs to the final customer. Those who suffer most are small-scale farmers in the Global South, who must compete with exports dumped on them. When they lose their farms, they may wonder if the $280-billion-a-year subsidy for cheap food might go instead to the 800 million people most at risk of starvation, thereby doubling their income and enabling them to buy food.[6]

Ray favors spending less money more wisely to pay farmers to 'set aside' marginal (too hilly or too sandy, and therefore prone to erosion) land and keep it out of food production. Ray also favors paying farmers for food reserves kept off the market and stored for a too-rainy or non-rainy day.[7]

In my opinion, supply management is not the most productive way to correct problems of cheap food, especially during an era of food shortages. Managing benefits creates more opportunities than managing supply, and that's the direction many people are moving in. Efforts are sprouting up to encourage farmers to produce more services – be they health, environmental, social or economic – and fewer but higher-quality commodities. These services are part of what used to be called the 'commons,' the original worldwide web of life. European Union farm policy-makers refer to these wide-ranging farm services as agricultural 'multi-functionality.' Innovative producer-consumer-government partnerships are exploring ways to pay food producers fees for public services – a way to use money now squandered on hidden costs of cheap food to create health, social and environmental benefits. The rise of Fusion is about this. 'The world doesn't change one person at a time,' say Margaret Wheatley and Deborah Freize. 'It changes as networks of relationships form among people who discover they share a common cause and vision of what's possible.'[8]

Economics

It's the economic services, stupid

Farms of the future will be classified as being in the service sector, not just the commodity sector. A good farm produces two kinds of services. There are environmental services. And there are economic, health and social 'distributed benefits.' If we can find ways to pay fair value for these services, farmers can earn a double dividend – a premium price paid by the customer for higher-quality foods, and a fee from the public for environmental services and distributed benefits. A rancher may get a good price for the rich taste and extra nutrients in grass-fed beef, for example, and then get a second check from agencies appreciating the enhanced water quality, and the new jobs in the tourism industry stimulated by scenic farm fields. Since producers get a second revenue stream from the general public, eaters only pay for food values. The rule about 'what goes around comes around' can bring good as well as bad news. The charge for creating social and environmental benefits will be spread over many beneficiaries, from water utilities that get cleaner water coming into their plants to hotels and restaurants that kick back part of the sales tax from tourists.

Although many countries base their general economy on services rather than farm or factory production, thinking about agriculture is still stuck in the olden days of commodity production. But eco-services have been the coming thing in farming since some 2,000 ecologists and scientific reviewers from 95 countries worked on the 2005 United Nations *Millennium Ecosystem Assessment Synthesis Report*. The birds and bees of the new farm economy come from seeing farms as public utilities that produce clean air and water and diverse green space, not just commodities.

The UN report reviews a range of otherwise-costly services farms can produce economically: storing carbon in the soil (by planting deep-rooted grasses, for instance) to reduce global warming; pre-cleansing river water for the nearby town water utility, providing habitat for birds and small animals (with hedgerows, for instance), and preserving genetic diversity of plants and livestock that might prove invaluable in the event of disease outbreaks. Unlike parks that feature the recreational value of landscapes, farmers can orchestrate 'working landscapes'. Calculating the economic value of such services is relatively straightforward. If high-quality river water lowers city costs for water filtration by a million dollars a year, local farmers can profitably be paid a million dollars a year for on-farm measures protecting water quality – planting trees or deep-rooted grasses near waterways, reducing pesticides, keeping livestock out of the river, and so on.

The report costs out the value of services from a hectare of Canadian marsh – storage and cleansing of water run-off, habitat for birds, cooling of the nearby area, for example – at $4,000 a year. By contrast, the value of food produced on the same hectare is $2,100. In a cheap food system which only pays farmers for food, the farmer will fill in the marsh and grow food on it, make $2,100 a year, and then beg for a subsidy from a general public that just paid out $4,000 for additional infrastructure to make up for the loss of marsh services. In a smart food system, the farmer will be paid $4,000 for services rendered by his physical plant, society gets $4,000 worth of services, and taxpayers face no taxes to cover farm subsidies.

Say it: market failure

The World Bank's annual report for 2008, *Agriculture for Development*, upholds the UN report's message. The 'new agriculture' will manage 'connections among agriculture, natural resource conservation, and the environment', the Bank says, as 'an integral part of using agriculture for development.' The Bank suggests that payments for environmental services 'can help overcome market failures in managing environmental externalities'. The taboo against talking about market failure has been broken. The World Bank report also recognizes that new farm stewardship methods – using trees to draw down nitrogen from the atmosphere rather than buying fertilizers, or using beneficial insects instead of pesticides to control pests, for example – will 'require more decentralized and participatory approaches, combined by collective action by farmers and communities'. Greens, fair traders and organic devotees are praised for including superior environmental services in their prices, and for their 'unique competencies' in delivering services at the community levels.

Aside from environmental services, farmers also produce public goods called 'distributed benefits', a term developed by energy gurus Amory Lovins and Paul

Whole lot of tradin' going' on

The Manifest Destiny of the US to feed the world did not pan out. The export:import ratio has stayed fairly stable through hot wars, cold wars, depressions, booms, subsidies and trade deals. Maybe it wasn't Manifest Destiny.

The great leap sideward of US food trade

Year	Agricultural Exports in Constant Billions	Agricultural Imports in Constant Billions
1935	0.67	0.93
1945	2.19	1.73
1950	2.99	3.18
1960	4.52	4.01
1970	6.96	5.69
1974	21.56	10.03
1981	43.78	17.34
1995	54.61	29.79
2006	68.59	64.03

Adapted from USDA, ERS, FY agtrade 1935-2007, YMS 1935 FY-1. xls; USDA, ERS, Value of US foreign trade and trade balance Jan-Dec 1992-2007; 'What Share of US Consumed Food is Imported,' *Amber Waves*, Feb. 08

Gipe. Social and economic benefits from local food production are often worth more to a local community than any money savings from cheaper long-distance food. Consider job creation. Local food comes with four sets of job magnets, all of which increase wealth in a community. First, farms create backward linkages, such as jobs making or repairing farm tools and barns. Second, farms can create forward linkages, such as an ice cream plant in a dairy district. Third, farms provide direct employment, maybe a summer job for a local student. Fourth, farmers create a 'multiplier effect' when they spend their earnings on a haircut or restaurant meal. Local food security is yet another distributed benefit, since local farms are a food lifeline in the event imports are blocked by an emergency with avian flu. Add the heritage value of old family farms and farm tours for local schoolchildren studying food-related topics, and the list of distributed benefits and likely contributors to the distributed benefits fund keeps growing.[9]

Few sectors can match food for distributed benefits. That's why it's such a false economy to select food exclusively on the basis of sticker price. The corporate chains that enforce and deliver cheap food come up short when it comes to the chain reactions that create a vibrant local business community. The deregulated free trade mania that has driven food policy since 1995 neglects as much as half the economic potential of food and farming. The emergence of Fusion-style consumers is starting to change that.

Buy the change you wish to see
The emergence of Fusion-style food initiatives coincided with the rise of consumer activism from the 1980s onwards. In the relatively affluent Global North, the two forces generated a rise in organic and fair trade sales that brought niche markets and market differentiation into the mainstream of food marketing.

That's an accomplishment, because food companies held out against the 'hundred channel universe' of consumer choice and diversity long after other industries embraced different, special and premium products. More recently, consumer activism and Fusion appetites have revived demand for local, ethical, healthy, ecologically responsible and slow foods from backyard and community gardens, farmers' markets and main streets occupied by neighborhood butchers, bakers and candlestick makers. As consumer power fans turn their attention to scaling up opportunities to create more local and sustainable production, they set their sights on public sector purchasing, likely to become a compelling issue of the coming decade.

The new consumer activists work with two tools. Boycotts try to save the world, one bankruptcy at a time. 'Buycotts' are a deliberate effort to support the likes of fair trade and organic producers. Boycotts have been directed against Nestlé for promoting formula feeding of infants in the Global South, where it is costly and unsafe to use because often there is no clean water to prepare it with. The consumer boycott of GE food has limited GE products to a few grains and oilseeds sneaked into processed foods; there are no 'GE inside' ads on processed foods. Buycotters protest in reverse by supporting those who allow them to buy things they need in a way that honors Gandhi's maxim to 'be the change you wish to see'.

Critics of consumer activism argue that activist shoppers simply ape the methods of a consumer culture, so overpowering that even opponents are reduced to new ways of shopping, rather than new expressions of citizenship. Critics also point out that boycotts are a tactic of the affluent, since people on low incomes can't afford more expensive options to cheap food. *The Economist* surprised many with a pre-Christmas broadside in 2007 on 'why ethical food harms the planet'. Where's Scrooge when you need him?

'The idea that shopping is the new politics is certainly seductive,' the editorial concedes. 'Never mind the ballot box: vote with your supermarket trolley instead,' scoff the champions of unregulated markets. 'Sadly, it's not that easy,' they say. 'People who want to make the world a better place cannot do so by shifting their shopping habits: transforming the planet requires duller disciplines, like politics.' The ethical food movement 'sends a signal that there is an enormous appetite for change and widespread frustration that governments are not doing enough to preserve the environment, reform world trade or encourage development,' say the Economistas. But 'if consumers really want to make a difference, it is at the ballot box that they need to vote.' Nothing makes free market enthusiasts change their tune faster than consumer engagement in market transformation.[10]

Buycotts work

Critics of buycotters might note that famous buycotts of the past used the positive energy of direct action to develop the economic and political muscle of a developing insurgency. During the Boston Tea Party of 1773, a shipload of tea from the British East India Company was tossed into Boston harbor to protest taxes imposed on American colonists. A buycott of coffee began, followed by the American Revolution a few years later. A few decades after that, Britain's anti-slavery movement, often described as the first mass movement of modern times, boycotted slave-grown sugar, then buycotted fair sugar, then succeeded in banning slave labor in the British empire.

In 1930, Gandhi led his first organized action to bid for India's independence – a march to protest British taxes on a local natural resource, salt. The point of Gandhi's campaign was to transform popular consciousness by empowering people to see and act on their right to access their own food commons, the ocean, for their own salt that could not be taxed by the British. Consumer action has rarely been the beginning and end of a matter, just the beginning.

Though the media often portray 'green business' as the way forward, not-for-profit green and social entrepreneurs are at least equally dynamic as a force for food innovation. Sometimes, non-profits connect farmers to customers who will shoulder the cost of additional benefits, as with fair trade coffee that delivers social and environmental improvements.

Sometimes customers, farmers and governments each pitch in, as when shoppers pay more for food from an organic farm that also gets a government fee to maintain farm hedges that feed and shelter birds and moles. Sometimes specific government agencies partner with farmers, as in Waterloo, Ontario, or New York City, where farmers receive fees to protect high-quality drinking water. Quite often, the 'third sector' of charities, non-profits and non-governmental organizations finds a funder to cover lost income from environmental stewardship, as when a nature conservancy group 'buys' the landscape services of a farm, forever prohibiting sale of those services to a shopping mall or subdivision.

The organic difference

Organics were the first Fusion-style foods to hit the market. During the 1970s, 'natural food stores' sold mostly nuts, dried fruit, brown rice, herbal teas and crunchy granola, a reflection of the narrow product base available. A short 20 years later, organics came full-on in supermarkets and neighborhood 'healthfood stores', stocking them with a full line of drinks, grains, fruits, veggies and meats, as well as frozen, canned and boxed prepared dinners. Organic versions of cosmetics, snack bars and pop tarts have been coming on strong since 2000, along with produce from around the world. The organic 'movement', as it still calls itself, has borne the brunt of angst about youthful idealism lost to the grinding logistics and harsh realities of tough customers who demand unblemished appearances, just-in-time delivery, steady volumes, long shelflife, convenient packaging and low prices.

Many early movement ideals and dreams have been compromised, to be sure. But progress has been steady on four fronts. First, brand equity has been built. 'Organic' is a diamond of a word, a shining and multi-faceted archetype of pastoral purity, natural goodness and wholesome integrity. Second, a steep learning curve has been climbed, and producers have taught themselves to grow, process and sell a full range of good-looking, good-tasting organic foods. Third, the demand for organic options forced mainstream retailers to open their doors to a challenging, high-quality, high-maintenance and premium line of foods that introduced niches to one of the last bastions of mass production uniformity. Fourth, organics held onto its price premium, a price point that comes close to the real costs of producing foods that respect human and environmental health.

Organic sales came on the mass-retail radar during the 1990s, a decade of internationally profiled food scares – mad cow disease was perhaps the best known – and worrisome innovations, such as genetic engineering. A new constituency of health-minded shoppers in North American and Europe came to organics. The new customers were less attuned to counter-culture values, and more concerned about allergies from additives and diseases from toxins.

Year after year, organic sales posted double-digit rates of increase, easily the fastest growth rate in the food industry. The new organic shoppers didn't know the farmers or processors making their food, and wanted some proof that premium prices were getting them more than good karma. That created pressure for strict certification, and eventually government-backed codes that enjoy consumer respect. While strict about production standards, the new customers were flexible about the organic product range. With few earth mothers back home to cook the organic ingredients from scratch for children who delight in simple whole-grained goodness, the real-life organic standard veered toward pre-packaged convenience.

'Economies of scope'

This consumer demand created an opportunity for conventional companies that have mastered the food industry's tricky wicket – what's called 'economies of scope'. Scope is what allows Nestlé to follow customers from cradle to grave, with formulas for every stage of life, and sales connections to match. Scope allows Coke to deliver a range of beverages to hundreds of thousands of supermarkets, corner stores and vending machines around the world. Food products are often sold by corporations that learned their business ethics selling tobacco, booze and soap, because they were the first products to require scope efficiencies in national and international markets.

Once a company has scope, it just adds products to its logistics chain. General Mills, Kellogg's, Mars, Heinz, Con Agra, ADM, Dole, Danone, Coke can swing both ways, conventional and organic. As they buy in, the organic 'market segment' begins to duplicate the corporate, long-distance and multi-ingredient supply chain of the conventional system.[11]

Nothing sucks like success, and many organic old-timers worry that two per cent of all food retail sales is dangerously far along the road to co-option. Several researchers have exposed a number of global food behemoths dipping their toes in the pure organic waters by buying out some respected organic companies.

To be realistic, this blip of a trend is the result, not the cause, of changes in organic retailing. If organic consumers bought only fruits, veggies, meats and bulk grains and beans, there would be virtually no corporate presence, just as there is virtually no corporate presence at farmers' markets or farm stands. But if organic customers want convenience packaging and non-seasonal foods, they're setting the stage for corporate players. Critics of corporate organic who want to confront system-wide drivers of corporatization should look in the mirror. Organic food needs organic customers who will change their shopping, cooking and eating habits as well as the certification of the food they buy. The two will co-evolve, like flowers and bees.

Solidarity consumerism

Fair trade foods and drinks have roared from a standing start in the 1990s to $2 billion in 2006 sales. Customers, mostly in the Global North, pay a premium price for coffee, tea, chocolate, dried fruit, bananas and similar products, expecting the premium to go to improved community services and better land stewardship (forest-grown coffee that protects migratory birds' nesting grounds, for example) in the Global South. As many as five million producers in over 30 countries benefit in some way from fair trade sales. In essence, fair trade shoppers pay the full price for needs and preferences neglected by cheap food – a delicious, bitter-free cup of coffee, a clear conscience after a treat, and the song of a favorite migratory bird that just flew in from a Global South farm.

As relationships are enriched, the distinction between fair and far foods may blur. Some fair trade imports might be seen as 'honorary local' foods, while some domestic foods grown and processed in disadvantaged conditions might be rewarded by fair trade premiums. The idea that Ethiopia's premium coffees might rate as honorary local foods intrigues Tadessa Meskela, general manager of the 102,000-member Oromia Coffee Farmers' Co-operative Union in southwestern Ethiopia and central figure in *Black Gold*, a gripping documentary about coffee workers.

If defining local food includes intangibles such as solidarity, quasi-tangibles such as 'terroir', as well as tangibles like embodied energy from field to plate, Meskela thinks his coffee is part way to local. That would ease the anxiety of locavores who can't get through a day without several hits of coffee – the second most-traded commodity in the world after oil. It would also relieve people in the Global South who rely on coffee and tea exports because their land (the mountains of Ethiopia, for example) doesn't support many other crops.

Turning coffee into a product that's co-produced close to where it's drunk is central to the new relationship with drinkers that Meskela hopes will benefit the world's 20 million impoverished coffee growers. 'We have to raise the education of the consumer,' he told supporters in Toronto during the fall of 2007. He's talking as much about educating the palate as the conscience. Few caffeine addicts know that low-caf, sweet, high-end Arabica coffees such as Sidamo come from Ethiopia, the birthplace of coffee, while harsher no-name placeless Robusta coffees were developed to meet the price point of corporate cheap food empires and low-end coffee chains.

Robusta jolted the coffee world during the 1990s, when the World Bank encouraged new countries to grow the (until then) decently priced crop, previously raised on bushes along hillsides and mountains. That World Bank initiative, together with its earlier opposition to co-operation among coffee-trading countries to manage supplies, swamped world markets with cheap Robusta coffee beans that drove coffee prices into the basement, condemning millions of growers to desperate poverty. On the other side of the coffee glut stood four corporations – Kraft, Nestlé, Procter & Gamble and Sara Lee. Monopolies used their purchasing power to demand prices as low as 40 cents a pound, says Anthony Wild, author of *Coffee, A Dark History*. Fair trade in foods (most products were crafts until that point) responded to this Bank-fostered economic tsunami.

Fair trade coffee

Teaching consumers to appreciate the taste, aroma and caffeine levels of Arabica coffee, Meskele hopes they will enjoy a drink that leaves no bitter residue among the people who grew it or the wildlife that cohabit coffee-rich mountains. He tours Europe and North America beating the bushes for community roasters who will partner to promote fresh-roasted coffee from fair trade Arabica beans. Meskele hopes new relationships will keep coffee growers from competing among themselves to sell to four or five global monopolies, and let them focus instead on finding their niche among hundreds of thousands of local roasters who sell fresh, artisan-roasted, naturally low-caffeinated coffee with no bitter aftertaste or rancidity. Such independent roasters and coffee shops will become anchors of main street hang-outs and neighborhood employment in the Global North while supporting thousands of prosperous coffee-growing villages.

Under what's called a 'slow trade' regime, green and durable coffee beans can be transported in bulk by ship and train, the lowest-packaging and least-polluting mode of transportation. That supply chain keeps the money close to where the value is added – growers and roasters. Since 2004, that approach to spreading the wealth has meant five elementary schools, five healthcare centers, 27 water-cleaning facilities, and two construction starts on new high schools in Oromia. If distributed benefits are valued, Meskele has found the mother lode. 'Trade has to work for the poor,' he tells me between slurps of cheap hotel coffee in a 6.00 am interview, before flying off to a trade show in Germany.

Economics

Fair trade towns

Especially in England, fair trade activists have stirred flair in their coffee by promoting fair trade towns and universities. The idea is that co-ordination makes it easier for individuals to flex their fair trade economic muscles on a regular basis. Garstang, Lancashire, in England was declared the world's first fair trade town in 2001. By 2007, Britain had 309, including London, Aberdeen, Leeds, Bristol and Nottingham. The European Union helps campaigners on the continent, where Rome is the star sign-up and Dutch and Scandinavian cities are joining quickly. North America is just starting.

A fair trade city makes some simple and practical commitments. The local council promotes fair trade, and serves fair trade products at City events. A nominal fee goes to fair trade co-ops in the developing world. There must be a minimum number of participating retailers and a campaign to increase their numbers. This is the spirit of getting started on 'continuous improvement'.

Malmö, a multicultural city of 270,000 in southern Sweden, shows how businesses, community groups and government agencies co-operate through this participatory democracy project. Malmö's campaign is led by a church, the Red Cross and a few unions. The Red Cross headquarters, Humanity House, features public exhibitions and talks, as well as a gift shop and café, 'where you can enjoy coffee and a cake with a clear conscience'. Lasting changes must start where people are at, Red Cross leaders explain. A city-funded directory of fair trade businesses trumpets the consumer's 'power to choose,' but notes that 'making an ethical choice is no longer for do-gooders but fashionable and fun.' The directory lists restaurants, gift shops, ice cream, clothing, furniture and grocery stores, as well as chains, discount stores, Pizza Hut and the Hilton. A Swedish-owned fairtrade coffee chain, Barista, is unionized, its owner says, 'because we believe in applying fair trade at home as well'. The city's website encourages tourists to live 'ethically and ecologically in Malmö,' with a variety of eco-gourmet tours and green golf courses.

'Fair to the Last Drop', a 2007 study by FoodFirst, calls such stepped-up versions of fair trade 'solidarity consumerism'. Such initiatives rely on what public health experts call 'environmental support', the kind of social marketing pioneered by anti-smoking advocates, but readily adaptable to food and drink. The idea is to encourage wise purchasing decisions by making them easier and more appealing for individuals and friends.[12]

Mindful, not judgmental

There's no need to wring hands about long-distance imports while sipping fair trade beverages. Use of buying power is about being mindful, not judgmental. Champions of local food such as Alisa Smith and JB Mackinnon, who base their delightful book on a year's experience eating only *The 100 Mile Diet*, use their storyline as a conceit, hooking people into the drama of their challenge with an otherwise mundane set of chores. But from the standpoint of pollution and global warming, embodied energy in transportation only accounts for 14 per cent of fossil fuels used in the food system. Nor is local food a diet, a word most people in the Global North automatically associate with food changes. The diet in the 100-mile diet is as much a stunt as the 100 miles. Sustainable foods require a system, not a diet, overhaul. And a good system design has to be balanced in terms of many elements it works with, including the ability of fairly paid plantation workers in distant lands to live more sustainably than they otherwise could. Fair trade can be a 'glocal' hybrid.

My favorite fair trade shopping expedition ever was

at Fabindia in downtown Mumbai, a long way from the stereotype that fair trade goods come from the Global South, but can't be sold there. One of India's most respected chain stores, Fabindia was founded in 1960 by US-born retailer John Bissell, who wanted to support India's village traditions in textiles. 'We believe that only fair trade will sustain these traditions in the long term,' the website says. Like the global fair trade movement, Fabindia started with village-crafted textiles and furniture during the 1960s, and expanded into food decades more recently, in 2004. Most foods are gift items (jams and honey, for example) and light meals sold in store cafés.

Quitting smoking

Bryan Gilvesy used to grow tobacco on his 140-hectare ranch in southwestern Ontario, but now raises Texas Longhorns, endangered prairie grasses, wild birds, restored woodlands, and clean, cold creek water safe for wild fish. Some of his customers pay him a premium price for his drug-free, free-range, energy-conserving, politically 100-per-cent correct beef. And then he has other customers – or maybe stakeholders, or investors, or partners or well-wishers – who pay him to grow back the endangered tall grass prairie that provides habitat for birds hatching their young, to keep the creek that flows through his land clean and cool, to stabilize the fragile sandy soils that he says 'can turn into a beach in a heartbeat' by restoring 50 hectares of hardwood forest.

Bringing this kaleidoscope of customers, stakeholders, investors, partners and well-wishers together is biologist Bob Bailey and an organization he helped found, called Alternative Land Use Services or ALUS. My wife used to worry when I told her I loved ALUS, the compulsive punster Gilvesy says. Lots of people love ALUS, including farmers looking for a way to get off tobacco, hikers, hunters, anglers, birdwatchers, environmentalists, charitable foundations and government water utilities. Some 300 people in the town of Delhi, population 5,000, turned up to cheer on Gilvesy when his ALUS project was formally launched in the harvest season of 2007.

On a haywagon ride around his farm, I check out the three hectares of tall grass prairie, which performs multiple functions. With roots that go five meters deep, the grass sucks down carbon from the air, which offsets global warming, stabilizes the sandy soil, lets rainfall percolate slowly so it doesn't flashflood into the creek, provides nesting grounds for birds, and even provides feeding grounds for patient Texas cattle. ALUS buys the prairie grass seed, and pays Gilvesy $400 a year to leave the field alone until mid-July, when the birds move on. The cattle are invited in for a feed, which Gilvesy says 'makes them fat and sassy', and ensures their beef is lean and well-priced. 'As I see it, society gets the use of my field for 10 months of the year, while I and my cattle only use it for two months,' he says, so it's fair that society pay its share of the overhead costs.

'We're where the water for this area is born,' Gilvesy says, so he works hard to keep it clean and cool, the way the fish need it to be, and the way the townsfolk like to have the water coming into their filtration plant. A variety of organizations, including the town water utility, give him a fee for his extra troubles to keep the creek clear and cool. ALUS also donates 30 bird boxes to house 60 bluebirds that eat crazy-making flies off the back of the Longhorns, saving Gilvesy the cost of spraying pesticides on their backs, keeping their bodies and the nearby creek pesticide-free.

At this stage, ALUS can pay Canadian farmers from $30 to $450 per hectare, depending on how much time they 'lose' on eco-service activity and the extent of eco-service they provide. ALUS is about as grassroots as prairie grass, which farmers like, since it protects them from high-handed government officials laying down the law on what form they must fill out to get their money.

Serious money

If governments could give up their control obsession and put in some serious money for public services that don't have an obvious user group, farmers would soon be in the eco-services industry. A leading economic thinker in this field, Pablo Gutman, estimates that three trillion dollars a year could be profitably invested this way, paying poor farmers around the world for non-food services that benefit the planet's soil, air, water, scenery and carbon storage. Trade food benefits, not food.[13]

A terrible tease but a lot of fun on a hayride, Gilvesy attracts a lot of people to his farm tours, and often ends up selling some beef direct, bypassing the middleperson. His meat is also certified by a local environmental organization, which earns him a premium at local restaurants. He loves his new career with ALUS.

'We used to be the people with a problem. Now, we're in the solutions business,' the former tobacco farmer says. 'Farmers can grow back wildlife habitat just like they grow any other crop. That's the sweet spot. It's win-win-win all over the place. I can say to the public "Now I work for you; just give me some support."'

Getting off the cheap food addiction to pollution and poverty doesn't have to be as hard as getting off tobacco.

Diabetic care

Kevin Morgan put down the newspaper article on Canada's runaway rates of diabetes, leaned across the breakfast table toward me, raised the furrow of his brow in that Welsh way, and whispered as if he was saying something seditious: 'Do you people not have a duty of care?'

I guess if careless driving, child neglect and professional misconduct are illegal, there must be a duty of care behind that, I said. But how does that relate to diabetes?

Well, the duty of care is all the rage in Europe, where the ills of obesity account for 10 per cent of health costs. Sooner or later, someone going through needless suffering is going to hire a lawyer to accuse politicians of sitting on their thumbs while their cheap food policies went out of control. Staying out of jail can be a powerful reminder of public duty. Morgan, an expert in government food purchasing at the University of Cardiff, told the conference we were both speaking at that the duty of care was helping create a 'new moral economy of food.'

Traditional government policy on food purchasing is determined by three factors, he says: cost, cost and cost. Allowable costs got so low that 'the kitchens and ovens went, and in came the scissors and microwaves' for opening and heating prefab food packages. Concern for health consequences led to accusations of being the would-be commissar of the nanny state.

'That accusation was the most spectacular innovation in the history of the food industry,' Morgan says. 'It had the same impact on (reform initiatives by) politicians as Kryptonite did on Superman.' But then came the duty of care, especially for the kids that nannies get paid to look after when parents aren't around.

Morgan developed the idea of the 'double dividend' of school meal programs. They can create benefits for student health and local jobs, he says. He was talking the language of Scotland's newly autonomous government, eager to launch a 'quality food revolution' that could overturn its record as the sick man of Europe. In 2002, before celebrity chef Jamie Oliver goaded the English Government, the Scots released a health

panel report called *Hungry for Success*. It favored a
'whole school approach' that encouraged nutritional
eating, socializing during meals, and learning about
food in classes. Parents were involved too. So were
school chefs, encouraged to experiment and reach for
the stars with seafood risotto, spicy Cajun wraps and
South African *bobotie*.

One school district in East Ayrshire, west of Glasgow,
took the *Hungry for Success* ball and ran, piloting a
Food For Life model promoted by the pro-organic
Soil Association. School purchases should be three-
quarters unprocessed foods (the cheapest and easiest
way to reduce salt, sugar and fat), half local, and 30
per cent organic. The county school program has won
national awards, acclaim and followers. This is grist
for the mill of Morgan's theories of the new economy
of disadvantaged areas, where 'civic capacity, public-
private partnership and a political leadership which is
honest and creative' step into the breach of do-nothing
central governments and lead people out of the cheap
food desert.

Non-food plus

The lawn in front of the student council center was
the launch pad for the University of Toronto's new
program to introduce local and sustainably produced
food to its 70,000 students – the largest student body
of any university in North America, and therefore the
largest local and sustainable food purchasing program.
The deal brings students together with farmers in the
world's largest – at 725,000 hectares – near-urban
greenbelt.

The new watchword for farmers and processors is
'local and sustainable'. Get used to those two formerly
distinct words rolling off the tongue together, with the
same mouth feel as macaroni and cheese, research and
development, health and wellbeing, equity and diversity, peanut butter and jam.

Local and sustainable is the new kid on the food block, taking on the junkfood juggernaut of distant and unsustainable, and edging up on distant and organic and local but unsustainable. Local Food Plus (LFP), which helped set the rules for the deal between the University of Toronto and food service companies, certifies farmers and processors who actively support local purchases and sales, animal and farm worker wellbeing, energy-efficient practices, safe pesticides, no-GE, and working landscapes respectful of biodiversity. (I'm happy to acknowledge that the person who invented and runs this organization is my wife.) The chemical use standards are less strict than organic, but the standards for social, economic and environmental sustainability are stricter. There's little latitude in such standards for the implicit standard of many change advocates, sometimes referred to as treating 'the perfect as the enemy of the good'. LFP standards for growers, purchasers and providers are based on continuous improvement or what public health types call 'harm reduction' – the longest journey begins with the first step, and slow and steady wins the race.

It certainly surprised me that a university would ever step up to the plate to use its purchasing power and prestige to put local and sustainable food on the map. But in a world of non-responsive institutions, post-secondary institutions stand out like a green thumb for being obliged to respond to students and faculty. Colleges and universities, often accounting for 10-20 per cent of local populations and economies, wield a lot of money and people power. If US universities were a country, they would be the 21st biggest economy in the world, Michael M'Gonigle and Justine Starke point out in their bracing book, *Planet U: Sustaining the World, Reinventing the University*. Universities, they argue, can and should use their purchasing power to set the standard for wages, building practices, waste management, and local, sustainable food in their communities.

Who's pulling the strings?

A university is as good a place as any to find distant power that's beyond control, pulling the strings of a cheap food system. Aramark, Sodexho and Compass: the Big Three food service companies come up again and again at universities, prisons, old-age homes, hospitals, corporate cafeterias, wherever there's a captive clientèle. (Giants such as Sysco and Gordon Food Service are as dominant in restaurants.) Though invisible to the public eye and most policy-makers, all five are as big as or bigger than most of the household names associated with Big Corporate Food.

Their power rests on a shaky foundation – disrespect for the food and non-food functions of food. Organizations such as universities and hospitals are highly specialized and purposeful, and they don't regard food as part of their business. Operating in organizational worlds where 'two priorities are no priorities', administrators are happy to dump food service headaches on someone else, unaware that food could be a defining force for good in their institutions. Not only do university students have a physical need for balanced and high-quality diets that meet their high-performance tasks, they have social needs that can be met by congenial student eating hang-outs. Food, in short, is central to the 'student experience'. It should be managed to achieve university and student goals, not contracted out. When that starts to happen, the corporate power that enforces cheap food will start to come undone.

I thought of this many times when I saw my wife leave her office in our basement to meet as an equal with representatives of multi-billion-dollar corporations. It reminded me of the *Wizard of Oz*, that barely disguised radical farm diatribe against the money power, the industrialists with no heart, and the politicians with no courage. But the all-powerful wizard, it turned out, turned into smoke and mirrors when confronted, since its power was power granted to it by people who might better have kept it themselves. The same wizardry keeps cheap food from being recognized.

1 M. Petticrew et al, 'Systematic review of the effectiveness of laxatives in the elderly', in *Health Technology Assessment*, Vol 1, No 13, 1997. **2** See www.foodforethought.net/By_Phil_Stuart_Cournoyer%P.S. Cournoyer%5B1%5D.pdf; P McMichael 'Book Review: The End of Poverty: Possibilities for Our Time', in *International Journal of Comparative Sociology*, Vol 46, No 4, 2005; 'Peasants Make their own History', (forthcoming). **3** J Pretty, *The Living Land: Agriculture, Food and Community Regeneration in Rural Europe* (Earthscan, 2001), p 78. **4** C Rocha, 'Food Insecurity as Market Failure: A Contribution from Economics', in *Journal of Hunger and Environmental Nutrition*, Vol 1, No 4, 2007. **5** EC Pasour, 'Intellectual Tyranny of the Status Quo', Econ Journal Watch, Vol 1, No 1, April 2004; M Pollan, In *Defense of Food: An Eater's Manifesto* (Penguin, 2008). **6** D Ray et al, *Rethinking US Agricultural Policy: Changing Course to Secure Farmer Livelihoods Worldwide* (Agricultural Policy Analysis Center, University of Tennessee, 2003); D Ray, 'A New Vision for Agricultural Policy', Presentation to the National Family Farm Coalition, Washington DC, 30 January 2005; H Schaffer et al, 'US Agricultural Commodity Policy and its Relationship to Obesity, Background Paper developed for the Wingspread Conference, March 2007. **7** D Ray et al, *Rethinking US Agricultural Policy: Changing Course to Secure Farmer Livelihoods Worldwide*. **8** M Wheatley and D Freize, 'Using Emergence to take Social Innovations to Scale,' www.evolutionarynexus.org/node/620, 2006. **9** A Lovins, 'Small is Possible: The Hidden Economic Benefits of Distributed Generation (and other distributed resources)', Rocky Mountain Institute, March 2002; P Gipe, *Community Power, The Way Forward* (Canadian Renewable Energy Alliance, August 2006). **10** T Smith, *The Myth of Green Marketing: Tending our Goats at the Edge of Apocalypse* (University of Toronto Press, 1998). **11** A Chandler, *Scale and Scope: The Dynamics of Industrial Capitalism* (Harvard University Press, 1990). For big business presence, see P Howard, 'Who owns Organic? From roots to suits', in *PCC Sound Consumer*, January 2007; V Cuddeford, 'When Organics Go Mainstream,' in Alternatives Journal, September 2003; M Sligh and C Christman, *Who Owns Organic? The Global Status, Prospects and Challenges of a Changing Organic Market* (RAFI-USA, 2003). **12** http://transfair.ca.en/fairtradetown; www.fair-trade.org.uk; www.malmo.se/turist/inenglish.4.33aee30d103b8f15916800021935.html **13** P Gultman (2007), 'Ecosystem Services: Foundations for a New Rural-Urban Compact' in *Ecological Economics*, Vol 62, Nos 3-4, 2007, pp. 383-387.

7 Somethin's gotta give

The industrial food system of the 1950s is well past its peak and cannot deliver affordable food in an era of expensive fossil fuels and degraded land, water and climate. When we understand this, we can see why system alternatives such as organics, agro-ecology and conservation will displace industrial food.

AS RECENTLY AS 2006, people such as Lester Brown of the Earth Policy Institute, Darrin Qualman of the National Farmers' Union of Canada and me were dismissed as alarmists when we warned that the end of cheap food was nigh. Never mind that world grain reserves were lower than any time since the 1970s, when food prices shot up almost as fast as oil, we were dismissed as cranky worrywarts in the tradition of Thomas Malthus, who predicted in 1798 that human populations would multiply faster than the food supply, but forgot, his critics like to scoff, that human ingenuity and technology can out-multiply anything. Defying Malthus and population bomb naysayers, the yaysayers liked to say, world population doubled to six billion between 1970 and 2000, yet the cost of meatier, milkier, sweeter, more exotic, processed, and convenient food stayed cheap and even declined in real dollars.

In affluent countries, food took up about 10 per cent of a family's income, a third of what families spent before World War Two, when the global Modernist food era was dawning. As the court jester of 1950s' Modernism, Alfred E Newman, used to say: 'What, me worry?' To this date, I'm not aware that any public health or safety official has insisted on a Plan B for any area in the event that global mishaps upset the apple-cart of imported foods – an omission that underlines the responsibility and governance vacuum in the food sector.

Halfway through 2007, the editor of *Food Navigator*, an electronic news service for industry insiders, surveyed the stats and ran a lead story on 'the death of the productionist model', which she described as the established way 'to feed as many people as possible as cheaply as possible by emphasizing quantity over all else'. She warned business bigwigs that cheap food was obsolete, and it was time to put on the thinking caps. By December, the dizzying rise of food prices became the story defining the year in review. The food price index kept by *The Economist* was at its highest since the magazine's founding in 1843, 75 per cent above price levels two years earlier, and a year-end edition ran a cover featuring stale toast under the headline, 'The End of Cheap Food'. Shortly after, Jacques Diouf, head of the FAO, got the news and called the swing in food prices 'unforeseen and unprecedented', and a calamity for the ability of the UN's World Food Programme to buy food for 78 million desperately hungry people.[1]

Food price hikes

Words like 'death of' and 'end of' are strong stuff, but food prices in 2008 live up to the billing: wheat jumped 287 per cent since 2006, corn 149 per cent, soybeans 129 per cent, rice 60 per cent. Some investment counselors called food 'the new oil', half investment bonanza, half disaster-in-the-making. Food scarcity is second only to the threat of nuclear war, said Bank of Montreal global portfolio manager Donald Coxe. 'We are facing the real possibility of the worst global food crisis for which we have records,' he says.

In poor areas of the world, where grain provides most calories, the cost of food imports in 2007 jumped 25 per cent. Riotous protests broke out in Mexico, India, Indonesia, Morocco, Yemen, Uzbekistan, Mauritania, Senegal and Burkina Faso. Governments in Egypt, India, Pakistan, Argentina, China, Thailand, Vietnam, Indonesia, Malaysia, the Philippines and Russia are subsidizing food costs for the poor or controlling exports or prices – almost unheard-of styles of government 'command and control' interventions since the deregulated 1990s.[2]

But headlines with 'death of' and 'end of' in them exclude choice and the possibility of making a difference. The actual food security challenge is not as severe as price hikes suggest. Abundant supplies of safe, healthy, environmentally friendly real food for all are within easy grasp, though the sources are not visible to Modernist eyes. Despite the ready existence of alternatives – a major theme of this concluding chapter – the pressures driving increases in food price levels will not let up any time soon. Nor are they a bad thing. High prices will not self-correct, because high prices are the corrective signal from the real world. If all the high-end food infrastructure stays – high fossil-fuel use, high rate of irrigation, high input costs for seeds, fertilizers, pesticides and farm machinery, high fat, high empty calories, high waste, high processing, high transportation, high packaging, high refrigeration, high subsidies, high medical costs, high pollution and high corporate concentration – the world will be locked into high costs for low-end food. Unless people combine personal, community and government initiatives to move in a new direction, an expensive cheap food system will emerge.

Challenges and opportunities

But price hikes signal new challenges and opportunities. For 50 years before 2007, the global cheap food system delivered cheap food globally, however much that conflicted with health, equity and environment. The land, water, seeds, nutrients, climate, crops, technology, farms and fisheries over-provided. As of 2007, however, the cheap food system is in conflict with its own 'system conditions', the factors that let it deliver. The world is about to rediscover Adam Smith's diamond-water paradox; diamonds are expensive and water is cheap, even though diamonds are frivolous and water is essential – so how will the value and price of water and food be determined when they are scarce and labor-intensive? Cheap food has not yet 'gone critical' with new questions because the new price level has not yet rocked either dominant institutions or popular understandings. One of those two factors has to come loose before there's a 'tipping point' in the discussion.

Nevertheless, a new pocketbook-informed hearing for Fusion food themes is on the menu. Until recently, any person proposing an end to cheap food and a turn toward higher food prices would have been labeled a misanthropic élitist. Since prices are up for the long term, a new dialogue can begin about new ways of producing and providing food, new ways of getting full value for money, innovative approaches for over-coming social inequities imposed by food prices that express real costs. There's not much choice but to think fresh. People running the old cheap food system couldn't figure out what to do when there was more food than they knew what to do with. They're still governing a situation where there is less food than they know what to do with. But somethin's gotta give.

The perfect squirm

I was hiding out to write this book at a friend's home in Santa Fe, New Mexico, when all the end-of-2007 stories on food prices broke. By chance, Miley Gonzalez, the state secretary of agriculture and chair of the North American Free Trade Area sub-committee dealing with farming regions, was bunk-ing in the same place. He offered to show me 'some real Mexican food' at Adelita's, where I was the only gringo in a restaurant named after heroines of the Mexican Revolution. Gonzalez encouraged me to try cow cheeks and lips, and see how people stretched food dollars by using cuts of meat that offended Anglo sensibilities. Gonzalez was in good spirits, because this spurt of 'agflation' was the first time in a long while he'd seen farmers make some decent money.

Though geography left New Mexico high and dry, it is a good time to be a farmer there. It has a reputation for adventurous eating, which plays well in today's world, where many people expect a meal to be a novelty. 'Other states have a state flower or bird, but we have a state question – red or green peppers,' Gonzalez tells me as we dig into some salsa that's immediately brought to the table to show hospitality. Salsa has trounced ketchup across North America, which raises demand for New Mexico's acclaimed chili peppers and onions.

It's also a good time to be farming close to Mexico and Central America. They typify the demographic changes reshaping the food world. First, as with most countries in the Global South, their numbers are growing at a rate that's leading to a 50-per-cent increase in world population, from just over six billion people in the year 2000 to nine billion in 2042. That's 80 million additional mouths to feed every year, with no corresponding increase in the size of the planet. Moreover, for the first time, more than half the world's people now live in cities, meaning more people than ever need to buy more of their food, another guarantee of strong food sales.

Young and hungry

With urbanization and industrialization comes a middle class with middle-class food tastes that's expected to swell globally to 1.8 billion people by 2020. And of course, all of the world's three billion new people will be young, in an age bracket when they eat parents out of house and home. Young people will be by far the biggest age-group in the Global South, unlike the North, where waist-watching 50-pluses dominate. Southern cities with lots of young families and middle-income earners are ideal for Northern fastfood chains and supermarkets, which feature the staples of a Northern meat and dairy-based diets.

This combination of increased population, increased urbanization, increased youth and increasingly rich foods will shape the demand on food for some time. People first saw how fragile and beautiful the planet looked from outer space during the late 1960s, an image that inspired Frances Moore Lappé to write her brilliant *Diet for a Small Planet*, warning that the emerging junk diet could not feed three billion people equitably while respecting the environment. How much less possible is it to feed nine billion equitably while managing the risks of a more fragile environment?[3]

Another population pressure that's raising demand for New Mexico's farm products relates to the rise of a billion or so middle-income earners among those who've migrated to cities in the Global South. Though plant-based diets are central to almost all folk food cultures, the new middle class wants to check out meat and dairy. This means demand for the grains and water that feed livestock will soar. Meat and milk are complex to raise, process, store and ship – which is why middlepeople prefer a food system based on them, rather than veggies that can come straight from the garden to the salad bowl or cooking pot.

People living in the cities of Mexico and Central America can't get local dairy products locally because on-farm refrigeration is rare; so the sales go to New Mexico, which Gonzalez is happy to say is fast becoming a dairy state, putting big demands on water, hay and grains, and pushing their prices up.

In China, per-person meat consumption has doubled over two decades. Asia also 'likes our protein', Gonzalez says. That adds to the pressure on demand for grains, which supply 70 per cent of the feed that livestock are raised on. It takes well over eight kilos of grain, for example, to produce one kilo of beef (the other seven kilos go to metabolism, horns, hooves, hide and manure). Meat is what creates the giant sucking sound for wheat, corn and soy, and explains why more grain has been eaten than grown since 2000, despite many record harvests. There was enough to feed the world for 18 weeks in 2005, and enough to feed the world for 12 weeks in 2007 – not reassuring to commodity speculators when the world's climate is going haywire, thanks to global warming and climate chaos.[4]

Biofuels

In the Global North, middle-income earners have long converted grain and water into meat and dairy; they now convert grain and water into fuel for their cars as well. Increased use of grains for transportation fuel is easily the most controversial of the factors driving up food costs. Defenders, such as the North American and European governments that subsidize ethanol production, claim that 'bio-energy' is a green substitute for fossil fuels, since the carbon burned in the gas tank is matched by the carbon drawn down by the growing plants.

Critics, including most environmentalists in Europe and North America, as well as the peasant organization Via Campesina, maintain that more fossil-fuel energy from fertilizers, pesticides and farm machinery goes into grain ethanol than comes out as fuel to drive cars. Critics also argue that it's unethical to use farmland to grow crops for cars while people go hungry. In 2007, UN human rights rapporteur Jean Ziegler, for instance, slammed grain ethanol as a 'crime against humanity'. The corn used up in 50 liters of car fuel could feed a child for a year, he argued, calling for a five-year moratorium on the project.[5]

When the debate about ethanol is linked to an analysis of the cheap food system, the friction generated by the ethanol debate comes across as displaced aggression. Whatever the problems with ethanol, wasting corn on ethanol (about 20 per cent of the US crop) is no worse than most uses of corn. About half the corn crop is used for livestock feed, used to fatten animals quickly because they fatten too slowly when they enjoy a free-range life munching on the food they evolved to eat – grass.

About five per cent of the corn crop is used for high fructose corn syrup, a cheap substitute for sugar that's used in soda pop, one of the more health- and environmentally destructive industries on the planet. Corn is the indispensable but phantom filler and fixer in most junk foods and drinks, as Michael Pollan shows in *The Omnivore's Dilemma*. Only about 10 per cent of a different variety of corn is grown to be eaten directly by humans, as corn on the cob, canned corn or cornflakes. The additional cost of a box of cornflakes after the price hike brought on by corn ethanol amounts to less than five cents. So the issue is not competition for the uses of corn. A human health and environmental discussion on corn would likely lead to phasing it out because it is so harsh on the land, requiring heavy machinery, fertilization, pesticide spraying, and reliance on GE seeds. The lack of controversy on that issue reflects the low level of agro-ecological understanding of food system issues.[6]

Farming futures

That said, the diversion of corn from junk food to car fuel illustrates the increasing convergence of food and energy in an era of fossil-fuel scarcity. This issue will decide the future of agriculture. Foodlands can be used to produce fuel, so food prices have to compete with fuel for access to the land resource; likewise, agriculture has to compete with cars, home heating and so on for access to fossil fuel-based inputs that get converted to nitrogen fertilizers and pesticides.

Somethin's gotta give

The entire energy equation, not just ethanol, needs a fresh look. Agriculture became as much a fossil-fuel industry as any heavy industry after the 1950s. An average North American or European farmer has as high a ratio of technology per worker as an auto or steel worker, and the capital equipment is just as dependent on fossil fuels to make and operate.

Natural gas makes nitrogen-based fertilizers tick, and petrochemicals help make pesticides kill. Without natural gas fertilizers, farmers wouldn't be able to grow the same crop on the same land year after year. They would need to rotate crops and animals in different years to replenish the soil's fertility. In an era which 'peakniks' define as one of 'peak oil' – when conventional (low-cost and easily accessible) fossil fuels have peaked, and

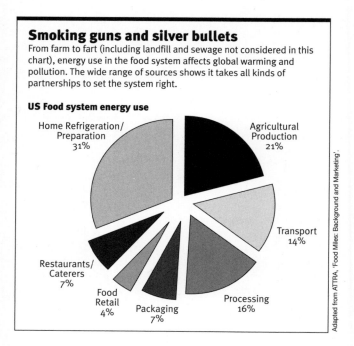

Smoking guns and silver bullets

From farm to fart (including landfill and sewage not considered in this chart), energy use in the food system affects global warming and pollution. The wide range of sources shows it takes all kinds of partnerships to set the system right.

US Food system energy use

- Home Refrigeration/ Preparation 31%
- Agricultural Production 21%
- Transport 14%
- Processing 16%
- Packaging 7%
- Food Retail 4%
- Restaurants/ Caterers 7%

Adapted from ATTRA, 'Food Miles: Background and Marketing'.

are being replaced by unconventional (high-cost and hard to access) fossil fuels – the food security challenge is to wean agriculture off fossil fuels and restore a solar-based system with as many efficient, energy-conserving and labor-using (humans are highly efficient users of energy, as those who try to take off weight by exercising can testify) technologies as possible. Far from hastening that process, corn-based ethanol locks agriculture into the fossil-fuel industry, reliant on fossil-fuel companies for farm inputs, and reliant on fossil-fuel gas stations to sell the car fuel.[7]

My dinner mate, Miley Gonzalez, understands this, which explains why he doesn't encourage a New Mexico version of corn ethanol. He sees a more sustainable future in local biofuels grown from local non-food crops. He's open to checking out algae, oil-rich plants that thrive in, and are thought to restore, ponds filled with livestock manure. He wants to pursue camelina, an ancient crop, sometimes known as wild flax or Siberian oilseed. An oil-rich plant, it is adapted to New Mexico's cool and dry climate, can be planted on marginal soils not suitable to other crops, and requires a bare minimum of energy-intensive tillage or weed control. Gonzales is also keen to try sunflower seeds, the protein from which can be used to feed livestock while the oil is siphoned off for fuel. Each of these options – in a different climate, hemp would be an option since one plant can be processed to extract food, fuel and fiber – accepts the agro-ecological proposition that complementary farming can produce fiber and fuel as well as food, and thereby contribute to a self-reliant and low fossil-fuel economy. This is where dialogue on the future of agriculture is heading, not to either/or deadlocks about corn ethanol.

Other pressures
Gonzales is also aware of the supply-side problems behind rising food prices, the side that most media

reports pass by. Demand-side aspects of rising food costs get covered – population increase, rise of meat and dairy sales, and so on. Supply presents more challenging problems. New Mexico's farmers and ranchers know first hand about the rainfall problems. 'Ranchers in New Mexico lost $900 million in 2002 and 2003 because of drought,' Gonzalez says. Access to water has become an ongoing global challenge to food security. Indeed, if environmentalists had been more food-positive, they might have relabeled global warming as global drying.

Global warming impacts moisture levels because additional heat evaporates more water from some areas and drops more of it elsewhere. Minor shifts in weather patterns can have a devastating impact because most of the world's prized 'breadbaskets' – the 'fertile crescent' in the Middle East, one of the birthplaces of agriculture; Mexico, another birthplace of agriculture; the Punjab of India and Pakistan, another birthplace of agriculture; and the western plains of North America spring to mind – are drylands never far from drought.

Drought attributable to global warming has already done grave damage to food production. Lack of rain took Australia, a major wheat exporter, out of commission in 2007. China's shortfall in 2007 wheat yield – equivalent to the entire Canadian harvest – was due to soil degradation and lack of water. Southeastern Europe's dry spell limited grain exports in 2006. By 2080, lack of moisture is expected to eliminate eight per cent of Africa's food-producing lands and 22 per cent of southern Asia's cereal-producing lands. A Stanford University study in 2007 tracked grain yields from 1989 to 2002, and found that every one-degree increase in temperature led to three to five per cent declines in yield, resulting in a 40-million-ton shortfall worth $5 billion over 13 years. That establishes one way to calculate the cost of failing to reverse global warming by phasing out fossil fuel use in farming and increasing storage of carbon in the land by growing more perennial crops.[8]

More than twin peaks

Converging peaks – peak oil, peak natural gas, peak soil, peak water, peak climate, peak invasive pests, peak fish, to name just the headline grabbers – are the new normal in food production. Fish, the main source of high-quality protein for the world's poor and health-conscious, may soon be the resource that got away. Fishing as if there was no tomorrow has all but finished the once-inexhaustible cod fishery off eastern Canada, the salmon fishery off the west coast of North America, and the North Sea off Britain. At least a quarter of commercial fish are at danger's door. Damage to corral-bed fish nurseries from high ocean acidity linked to global warming jeopardizes the future.

Cheap fish degraded the physical habitat of fisheries and farms, and also the social habitat, the communities that raise and support food producers. As part of his committee work with NAFTA, Gonzalez is keenly aware of that challenge. The lurch in food prices 'puts the need to restore the vitality of rural communities across North America and Mexico back on the agenda,' he says. Restoring a place doesn't happen as quickly as planting a different crop for a higher price, he tells me, as I nurse the cow lips and cheeks Gonzalez encouraged me to try, poking away at a folk tradition that found a use for every part of an animal, not just the expensive cuts. I see that culture and community will need to be part of the solution to future food production strategies.

Diet for a mindful planet

Food production needs a system redesign to outfit it for today's and tomorrow's needs. I'm not going to try to outline that in a few concluding pages. Instead,

Somethin's gotta give

I want to emphasize the importance of building from strengths, and identifying low-hanging fruit so that specific projects meet an objective and develop a sense of momentum and success that lead to other projects. If we're honest about the situation we face, and the strictly emerging status of most food innovations, starter kits are the need of the hour.

Initiating community and government payments for farm-produced environmental goods and services is a priority to anyone who understands the centrality of the climate protection challenge, and who is looking for ways to encourage farmers on low incomes to feed themselves while earning extra income from environmental fees.

To build from strength: new evidence confirms that organic methods can nourish the world more effectively than high-input methods. Jules Pretty, a sustainable agriculture expert from Essex University in England, was the first to work up some hard global numbers on organic farming. His 2001 study, *Reducing Food Poverty with Sustainable Agriculture: A Summary of New Evidence*, reviews 208 innovative farm projects by nine million farmers in 28 countries. In the previous decade, impoverished farmers on smallholdings jacked up the amount of land under earth-friendly stewardship by an astounding 28,000 per cent, from 100,000 to 29,000,000 hectares. The greatest increase in farm productivity, Pretty found, came from working to increase a 'sustainability dividend' by paying attention to 'natural' and 'social' capital.

When fish are raised in rice paddies, Pretty discovered from a typical case, there's a health, environmental and economic dividend. The fish eat insects that would otherwise prey on rice and spread malaria to rice paddy workers. The fish also enrich the soil with their excrement. Then they provide protein to the farmers. This kind of 'virtuous circle' can replace the 'vicious circles' of chemical farming methods, Pretty argued.

Low-resource farmers

In 2007, two reports added heft to Pretty's overall findings. At a May 2007 conference sponsored by the FAO, Dadia El-Hage Scialabba highlighted the accessibility of organic methods. Non-organic methods may produce higher yields, she said, but peasants and smallhold farmers can't afford the expensive inputs (hybrid seeds, fertilizers, and so on), and cannot get to a nearby market to sell any surplus produce. Organic methods require labor rather than cash purchases, and are therefore better suited to what low-resource farmers can afford, she said. Ability to make use of local, low-cost and natural assets such as animal manure is 'the strongest feature of organic agriculture', Scialabba claimed. Later that year, Ivette Perfecto from the University of Michigan published her evaluation of 293 case studies, which showed that an organic world could yield over 2,641 calories per person per day. Her study also confirmed that small farms are the most productive, good news if farming is to provide healthy careers for hundreds of millions of the world's job-seekers. When carbon exchanges and other methods for financially rewarding people who store carbon in the soil are functioning, peasants and farmers following organic methods will have two benefit streams: food for themselves and perhaps surplus for sale, and income from the sale of carbon credits rewarding them for soil enhancements that store more carbon underground.[9]

How green is my alley

Urban agriculture once seemed as illogical as military intelligence or Microsoft Works. But in a world that is 50 per cent urban, it has a role to play. Moreover, urban agriculture almost defines what multi-benefit projects are about. Food is only one product of an urban farm; others include environmental education, community development, resource and waste management, personal skill and esteem building, employment readiness training, fitness and nutrition. There are so many benefits and paybacks that every municipality should have at least one animator on staff to help people organize and start gardens.

From Saskatoon, Saskatchewan, comes SPIN farming, which stands for Small Plot Intensive farming, developed by Wally Satzewich, who farms in 25 backyards donated by well-wishers. Someone with a dream to be a professional gardener, but without the means or desire to own a big rural farm, can take advantage of the city's easy contact with potential customers, ample compost, water hoses, walls that provide wind breaks and other season extenders that permit two crops a year, and produce a large variety of niche products that fetch a good enough price for a decent life.

Retired basketball star Will Allen, founder of Growing Power in Milwaukee and Chicago, has a more complex operation. He manages 19 employees and a hundred volunteers who work in six greenhouses linked to a food retail outlet, commercial kitchen, livestock and beekeeping operation on the outskirts of Milwaukee, close to an Afro-American neighborhood Allen serves and recruits from. Allen and I are on the board of the Community Food Security Coalition, and he gave me a tour in 2004 that showed off the scrap wood, found clothes dryer, donated food scraps, volunteers and sheer grit behind Growing Power, which is about teaching kids from the nearby Afro-American neighborhood to 'keep coming back and not quit. The most powerful thing about this place is that people can come and see it, and leave ready to pick up a shovel and do it.'

The power source for the business is the second greenhouse, which houses the compost. Every week, Allen gets 2,000 kilograms of mash from an organic brewery, 500 kilos of coffee grounds from local restaurants, and tons of fruit and veggies that arrived at local food banks too late to be edible. This is Allen's money machine. Composting throws off enough heat to keep the greenhouses warm through Milwaukee's freezing winters. Huge bins are breeding grounds for tens of thousands of worms that break down the food scraps and produce castings that go into compost teabags called Milwaukee Black Gold. A bin's worth of tea bags sell for $36,000. 'It would take a rancher 300 steers to equal the value of my worm livestock,' Allen says, a six-foot seven-inch gentle giant who loves to fondle his red wrigglies in his hands.

Herbal leasing

His other livestock dominate the fourth greenhouse, where a 16,600-liter container hosts 4,000 tilapia, small fish that evolved in the shallow and still waterways of Africa and Asia. For about eight months, the fish eat algae, water lettuce, duckweed (39 per cent protein) and worms, all grown in the complex, before they reach their final weight, about two-thirds of a kilo, and are sold for meat. Allen turns that eight-month waiting period into a revenue stream by channeling tilapia excrement and compost tea to hydroponic trays that feed a wide range of herbs and greens, including watercress, cilantro, basil, eddo and baby bok choy. About 5,000 pots of herbs grow in the enriched water, ready to be shipped to local chefs who clip fresh sprigs of herbs just before they serve meals. Chefs lease their pot of herbs for $50 a month, then return them for another.

The last greenhouse has raised beds where salad greens are planted thickly along hills of compost. The salad greens have their own pup tent to hold the heat from the ground and compost, so no other heat source is needed to get them through the winter. Outside the greenhouse are goats, rabbits, duck, chickens and bees that produce 300 kilograms of honey from white clover in nearby fields.

Somethin's gotta give

Allen's hope is to show that a producer on one acre (0.4 hectares) of land, humming with 'closed loop' systems that convert 'waste' into a resource, can provide 1,000 people with healthy and affordable food basics. He estimates that once a system is ramped up, one person can make a decent income from one acre.

The brown agenda

It's not much different in Sri Lanka or Uganda. 'It's all about the brown agenda,' says Luc Mougeot, as he bounds up a stairwell to the workshop with city farmers from Sri Lanka, Argentina and Uganda. Seeing my eyes glaze over, Mougeot explains that the brown agenda came out of the United Nations Agenda 21 of 1992. It's about redeeming and converting urban waste, such as dishwater, rainwater and food scraps, into a resource for food production. In an ideal scenario, the farmer would be paid twice, once for getting rid of garbage, and once for growing food. Mougeot and his unit at Canada's International Development Research Centre hosted a 2005 workshop at Montreal's McGill School of Architecture to design low-cost homes for city farmers, and I was invited to speak to them.

Colombo's chief medical officer, Dr CD Palathiratne, works with people in the shantytowns, where 46 per cent of the population crowd onto 12 per cent of the land – 'squatting' near floodplains, garbage dumps, refineries or power lines. Access to running water, flush toilets, sewers or green space is rare. Dr Palathiratne promotes city farming to provide income opportunities for women, low-cost nutrition for families, and herbal remedies in the Ayurvedic healing tradition. He encourages shantytown squatters to grow five plants rich in protein, minerals and vitamins – ginger and wild asparagus are the most recognizable to Westerners – that can creep up walls and fences, handle the cramped quarters of windowsills, or thrive in baskets hanging from roofs or containers resting on ledges. Some of the leaves are ground into porridge and cooked up as survival food to prevent malnutrition. Some leaves are bought by the city, processed in 20 city dispensaries into herbal medicines, and given free to the poor when they're sick, saving the medical system from paying for expensive imports of Western pharmaceuticals.

Colombo's city planners follow the same 'hope-giving approach' to engage shantytown residents in 'community action planning', he says. They work with residents to compost waste water and 'humanure' (human excrement) for food production, thereby keeping them from contaminating water supplies, a major cause of illness in the Global South.

That's the combination Mougeot is looking for. 'I'm as interested in the inputs for urban agriculture as the outputs,' he says, a reference to the fact that city crops can be irrigated with washwater and fertilized with composted humanure, while city livestock can convert kitchen food scraps into protein and manure that produces biogas energy. Waste water, food scraps and humanure fit the definition of pollution as 'good resources in the wrong place', since the problem is not with them, but the fact that there's no place to put them to work in the farmless city. By keeping together the whole life cycle of agriculture, 'urban agriculture is a way to make cities more efficient in the way they use resources,' says Mougeot. This kind of agricultural multi-tasking deserves brownie points in a world that's over half-urban.

Waste not, want not
When something is priced too cheap, it is often wasted. And so it is with food in the Global North. Wasted food is not only a benefit lost. It is harm done, as when tossed food ends up in landfill, where goo sinks and poisons water tables and where rot turns into methane, with 22 times more global warming effect than

carbon dioxide – methane which can almost effort-lessly be harvested from landfills as a clean-burning fuel akin to natural gas. In the Global North, perfectly good but undervalued foods and food byproducts are wasted that could more easily provide positive func-tions and address global warming reduction targets. Every municipality should convert its waste manage-ment department into a resource recovery department; preparing for that, a team should be assigned the task of identifying revenue-generating or environmentally beneficial recovery projects.

Such are the teachings of Vaclav Smil, leading geog-rapher and author of *Feeding the World: A Challenge for the Twenty-First Century*. 'Our response to higher demand should not be primarily the quest for higher supply through increased inputs, but rather the pursuit of higher efficiency,' he writes. 'Higher conversion effi-ciencies are our best prevention and defense' against shortages. Smil is befuddled by the fixation he sees with improving farmer or fisher productivity, with hundreds of millions spent to jack up production by one per cent. Yet he sees no attention to increasing productivity in waste – or rather, resource – management.

A little care in post-harvest handling could end the wasting of 10 per cent of cereals, more than 25 per cent of spoiled fruits and vegetables, and even more fishery 'bycatch', valuable fish tossed overboard because the crew isn't paid to bring them back. 'We should look for more food not only in fields, pastures, barns and ponds but also in storage bins and sheds, in warehouses and supermarkets, in food service and in household pantries and refrigerators,' Smil argues. 'And, no less importantly, in our eating habits – and in scientific understanding of our nutritional needs.' Despite all the institutions fretting about increased production, he notes, 'We do not have even a single organization devoted to the worldwide problem of food losses.'

Cosmetically challenged foods

Smil estimates that the energy and nutrient equivalent of 100 megatonnes of grain a year, 'nearly half of all cereals on the world market', could be conserved if the 'rich world' reduced its overall waste by 20 per cent. In my experience, that would be a snap. When I and my family do a stint of volunteering on organic farms each summer, we usually spend the hottest hour of the day culling the items that can't be sold. Nothing is wrong with these items from the standpoint of safety, nutrition or taste. They just don't look the way they do in the food fashion magazines. The carrots don't have the shape of a Barbie Doll. The onions or garlic have a blotch on their skin. The apples are too small, the salad leaf a little torn. They are all cosmetically challenged. About a third of the fruits and vegetables grown in North America don't get to the store because of this. If the farm has staff and volunteers who know better, they can enjoy a feast of 'farmie food,' as we called it. If a farm is diverse, the scrapped foods can be fed to chickens and pigs, who don't discriminate on the basis of superficial appearances.

For the most part, however, a third of many farm foods are lucky to be used for compost. Similar culls take place at processors and supermarkets. A screw-up in labeling or packaging ends up as garbage. When dairy products get close to their best before dates – what customer wants to buy milk on 5 June that may go off on 8 June, and what retailer wants to keep the brand-new shipment of milk in storage until the old stuff has sold? – the milk is tossed. Home waste is at least as bad. Standard estimates for consumer wastage in the Global North are in the 25 to 40 per cent range.[10]

Food banks in the Global North try to reclaim a small portion of packaged items that store easily to give as charity for the poor. Linking waste management to poverty alleviation is the low end of food conservation. Instead of wasting the opportunity to help build esteem, personal skills and social connections, the millions of volunteers at Global North food banks would be doing the world a much bigger favor, Mark Winne has argued in *Closing the Food Gap*, by campaigning for adequate incomes to make safe, nutritious food affordable and to promote personal and community self-help projects such as community gardens and community kitchens.[11]

Most of the ecosystems on Planet Earth yield abundance – if not to humans, then to other creatures. Making more mindful use of such potential requires eyes trained to spot 'unused capacities', the most productive resource in the world – like the kitchen scraps that heat Will Allen's greenhouse, then get sold as compost tea bags. It is humble work, partnering with other people and with natural processes – not exactly the swashbuckling and conquering humans many pictured during the heyday of 1950s' Modernism, described in the first chapter. Food is most challenging to people with a Modernist upbringing because warming to food is about warming to this humility, this awareness of the oneness and connectedness of, and responsibility to, all beings. This is what food system redesign is nurtured by and grows on. It's hopeful, it's positive, it's fun, it's meaningful, however partial the success. And it reveals the wisdom, radicalism and militancy behind an old saying I always hated until I worked in food causes: blessed are the meek, for they shall inherit the earth.

1 Navigator.com, 9 April 2007; *Time*, 21 June 2007; *The Economist*, 1 December 2007, p 113; *The Economist* 8 December 2007, p 11; E Rosenthal, 'World food stocks dwindling rapidly, UN warns', *International Herald Tribune*, 17 December 2007. **2** D Olive, 'Agriculture's New Golden Age', *Toronto Star*, 2 March 2008; *Globe and Mail*, 15 February 2008; 15/08; Economic Research Service/USDA, 'The Influence of Income on Global Food Spending', in *Agricultural Outlook*, July 1997; *Guardian*, 26 February 2008; 'The World's Growing Food-Price Crisis', in *Time*, 27 February 2008; 'Rice now too costly to give away', *Asia Times*, 6 March 2008; 'Rising Food prices Intensify Food Insecurity in Developing Countries', in *Amber Waves*, February 2008. **3** On world population and country surveys, see US

Census Bureau, International Data Base; see also David Foot's collection of statistics in www.footwork.com; on rising middle class, see M Naim, 'Can the World Afford a Middle Class?', in *Foreign Policy*, March-April 2008; on dairy, see Business Day, 16 May 2007; on supermarkets and dietary change, see 'Converging Patterns in Global Food Consumption Food Delivery Systems', *Amber Waves*, February 2008. **4** C Gillis, 'Why your grocery bill is about to hurt', in *Macleans*, 10 March 2008. **5** 'UN Rapporteur calls for biofuel moratorium,' Swissinfo.org, 11 October 2007; G Monbiot, 'Agricultural Crime against Humanity', *The Guardian*, 6 November 2007. **6** 'Corn Prices Near Record High, but what about food costs', in *Amber Waves*, February 2008. **7** See autoblog, Pro-ethanol-folks-respond-to-Economist's-ethanol-attack.htm for a wide range of comments and sources on ethanol and food prices. **8** On supply-side shortages, see 'China yearly shortfalls in wheat ...' AP-Foodtechnology.com 8 October 2007; 'Global Production Shortfalls Bring Record Wheat Prices', in *Amber Waves*, November 2007 ; J von Braun, *The World Food Situation: New Driving Forces and Required Actions* (International Food Policy Research Institute, December 2007); 'Development: Food Prices Climbing With No End in Sight', *Inter Press Service*, 5 December 2007; Reuters, 19 March 2007, posted Rachel's Democracy and Health News, 899, 22 March 2007; 'Australia drought hit world's third largest wheat exporter and key supplier...,' *San Jose Mercury News*, 16 March 2007; 'The big dry,' *The Economist*, 28 April 2007, pp 81-2. **9** I Perfecto, 'Organic Farming Can Feed the World (Part 1), http://www.organicauthority.com/blog/?p=514. **10** For sample reports on waste, see www.telegraph.co.uk/news/main.jhtml;jsessiond=LEKFS 1AC5UF1BQFIQMGCFFOAVCBQUIXML=/news/2007/03/17/nfood7.xml ; L Heller and J Luesby, 'Arizona study finds we waste half of food we produce,' *Agribusiness Examiner*, 16 August 2005; Organic Consumers Association, 'US Wastes $14 bill in Food and Crops Every Year,' 20 June 2005, www.knoxstudio.com/shns/story.cfm?pk=GARBAGE-08-10&cat=an; *Sustainability Planning News*, 18 March 2007; 'Britain Wastes as Much as Half the Food it Produces', terradaily, 3 March 2008. **11** M Winne, *Closing the Food Gap: Resetting the Table in the Land of Plenty* (Beacon Press, 2008).

Contacts and resources

Action Group on Erosion,
Technology and Concentration
www.etcgroup.org

American Community Gardening
Association
info@communitygarden.org

City Farmer News
cityfarm@interchange.ubc.ca
www.cityfarmer.info

Community Food Security Coalition
aleta@foodsecurity.org
www.foodsecurity.org

Development Alternatives with
Women for a New Era
info@dawnnet.org
www.dawnnet.org

Fairtrade Foundation
mail@fairtrade.org.uk
www.fairtrade.org.uk

Federation of City Farms and
Community Gardens
www.farmgarden.org.uk

FIAN International
www.fian.org

Food and Agriculture Organization
www.fao.org

The Food Commission
enquiries@foodcomm.org.uk
www.foodcomm.org.uk

Food First
info@foodfirst.org
www.foodfirst.org

Foodforethought
editor@foodforethought.net
www.foodforethought.net

FoodShare
info@foodshare.net
www.foodshare.net

Friends of the Earth
www.foe.co.uk

Institute for Agricultural and Trade
Policy
iatp@iatp.org
www.iatp.org

International Institute for
Environment and Development
mail@iied.org
www.iied.org

Metcalf Foundation
info@metcalffoundation.com
www.metcalffoundation.com

Ministry of Agriculture Sustainable
Farming Fund New Zealand
www.maf.govt.nz.sff

The Oakland Institute
info@oaklandinstitute.org
www.oaklandinstitute.org

Oxfam UK
enquiries@oxfam.org.uk
www.oxfam.org.uk

Permaculture Research Institute of
Australia
tom@permaculture.org.au
www.permaculture.org.au

Portal for the Promotion and
Protection of the Rights of Migrants
info@december18.net
www.december18.net

Seeds of Diversity:
mail@seeds.ca
www.seeds.ca/en.php

Slow Food International
international@slowfood.com
www.slowfood.com

Stop Community Food Centre
general@thestop.org
www.thestop.org

Sustain
sustain@sustainweb.org
www.sustainweb.org

Toronto Food Policy Council
tfpc@toronto.ca
www.toronto.ca/health/tfpc_index.
htm

Women's Environment and
Development Organization
wedo@wedo.org
www.wedo.org

World Health Organization
foodsafety@who.int
www.who.int/foodsaefty/en/

World Hunger Year
media@worldhungeryear.org
www.worldhungeryear.org

World Wide Fund (WWF) Australia
www.wwf.org.au/ourwork/indus-
try/agriculture/

Index

Index

Index

Index

Index